DISCOVERING CAREERS FOR YOUR FUTURE

environment

Ferguson
An imprint of Infobase Publishing

Discovering Careers for Your Future: Environment

Copyright © 2008 by Infobase Publishing

Ferguson
An imprint of Infobase Publishing
132 West 31st Street
New York NY 10001

Library of Congress Cataloging-in-Publication Data

Discovering careers for your future. Environment.
    p. cm.
   Includes bibliographical references and index.
   ISBN-13: 978-0-8160-7281-1 (hardcover: alk. paper)
   ISBN-10: 0-8160-7281-7 (hardcover: alk. paper) 1. Environmentalists—Vocational guidance—Juvenile literature. I. J.G. Ferguson Publishing Company.
   GE60.D57 2008
   333.72023—dc22
                                                    2007040858

Ferguson books are available at special discounts when purchased in bulk quantities for businesses, associations, institutions, or sales promotions. Please call our Special Sales Department in New York at (212) 967-8800 or (800) 322-8755.

You can find Ferguson on the World Wide Web at http://www.fergpubco.com

Text design by Mary Susan Ryan-Flynn
Cover design by Jooyoung An

Printed in the United States of America

EB MSRF 10 9 8 7 6 5 4 3 2 1

This book is printed on acid-free paper.

Contents

Introduction

You may not have decided yet what you want to be in the future. And you do not have to decide right away. You do know that right now you are interested in the environment. Do any of the statements below describe you? If so, you may want to begin thinking about what a career in the environment might mean for you.

___Environmental science is my favorite subject in school.
___I like teaching people about nature and the environment.
___I am concerned about preserving endangered species.
___I love being outdoors.
___I am interested in learning more about renewable energy.
___I am active in recycling projects.
___I like to study the plants and trees native to my area.
___I worry about air, water, and soil pollution.
___I participate in community clean-up projects.
___I like to discuss environmental issues with friends and family.
___It upsets me to hear about events like oil spills or global climate change.
___I enjoy learning about the weather.
___I enjoy taking trips to state and national parks with my family.

Discovering Careers for Your Future: Environment is a book about environmental careers, from air quality engineers and foresters to marine biologists and soil scientists. People in environment-related careers are interested in and deeply concerned about how humans interact with and change our planet. They study the Earth and seek ways to reduce pollution, save land from development, utilize renewable energy resources, and conserve natural resources.

This book describes many possibilities for future careers in the environment. Read through it to learn about the variety of careers that are available. For example, if you are interested in animal life, you will want to read the chapters on marine biologists, oceanographers, and park rangers. If you are interested in ecology or conservation, you will want to read the chapters on ecologists, foresters, land trust or preserve managers, soil conservationists and technicians, and soil scientists. If you are interested in business or law as it relates to the environment, you will want to read the chapters on environmental lobbyists and land acquisition professionals. Go ahead and explore!

What Do Environmental Workers Do?

Each chapter begins with a heading such as "What Environmental Engineers Do" or "What Energy Conservation Technicians Do." This section tells what it's like to work at this job. It also describes typical responsibilities and working conditions. Which environmental professionals work in forests or beneath the ocean's surface? Which ones work at computers in offices? Which work in the halls of Congress? This section answers these and other questions.

How Do I Become an Environmental Worker?

The section called "Education and Training" tells you what schooling you need for employment in each job—a high school diploma, training at a junior college, a college degree, or more. It also talks about what high school and college courses you should take to prepare for the field.

How Much Do Environmental Workers Earn?

The Earnings section gives the average salary figures for the job described in the chapter. These figures give you a general idea of how much money people with this job can make. Keep in mind that many people really earn more or less than the amounts given here because actual salaries depend on many factors, such as the size of the company, the location of the company, and the amount of education, training, and experience you have. Generally, but not always, larger companies located in major cities pay more than smaller ones in smaller cities and towns, and people with more education, training, and experience earn more. Also remember that these figures are current or recent averages. They will probably be different by the time you are ready to enter the workforce.

What Will the Future Be Like for Environmental Workers?

The Outlook section discusses the employment outlook for the career: whether the total number of people employed in this career will increase or decrease in the coming years and whether jobs in this field will be easy or hard to find. These predictions are based on economic conditions, the size and makeup of the population, foreign competition, and new technology. Terms such as "about as fast as the average" and "slower than the average" are used by the U.S. Department of Labor to describe job growth predicted by government data.

Keep in mind that these predictions are general statements. No one knows for sure what the future will be like. Also remember that the employment outlook is a general statement about an industry and does not necessarily apply to everyone. A determined and talented person may be able to find a job in an industry or career with the worst outlook. And a person without ambition and the proper training will find it difficult to find a job in even a booming industry or career field.

Where Can I Find More Information?

Each chapter includes a sidebar called "For More Info." It lists resources that you can contact to find out more about the field and careers in the field. You will find names, addresses, phone numbers, e-mail addresses, and Web sites of environment-oriented associations and organizations.

Extras

Every chapter has a few extras. There are photos that show environmental workers in action. There are sidebars and notes on ways to explore the field, fun facts, profiles of people in the field, and lists of Web sites and books that might be helpful. At the end of the book you will find a glossary, an index, and a Browse and Learn More section. The glossary gives brief definitions of words that relate to education, career training, or employment that you may be unfamiliar with. The index includes all the job titles mentioned in the book. The Browse and Learn More section lists environmental books and Web sites to explore.

It's not too soon to think about your future. We hope you discover several possible career choices in the environmental field. Happy hunting!

Air Quality Engineers

What Air Quality Engineers Do

Air quality engineers, also called *air pollution control engineers*, develop ways to analyze and control air pollution. Clean air is necessary for healthy living and is protected by U.S. government laws. Air quality engineers help manufacturers and cities meet those federal requirements.

Many industrial and fuel-burning processes produce waste through exhaust or evaporation, called emissions. This is part of the cause of air pollution. For example, the carbon monoxide released from automobiles and manufacturing factories is a major air pollutant.

Indoor air can become polluted, too. Poor ventilation in a polluted building can create serious health issues for those working or living in it. This problem is known as "sick building syndrome." Air quality engineers must determine the cause of the pollution in the building and work to get rid of and reverse its effects on the building's inhabitants.

Air quality engineers work in several types of jobs. Some air quality engineers work for manufacturers. They monitor the level of harmful pollutants in their company's emissions. They might evaluate and suggest changing parts of

U.S. Metropolitan Areas with the Best Air, 2007

1. Cheyenne, Wyoming
2. Santa Fe–Española, New Mexico
3. Honolulu, Hawaii
4. Great Falls, Montana
5. Farmington, New Mexico
6. Flagstaff, Arizona
7. Tucson, Arizona
8. Anchorage, Alaska
9. Bismarck, North Dakota
10. Albuquerque, New Mexico

Source: American Lung Association (by degree of long-term particle pollution)

U.S. Metropolitan Areas with the Worst Air Pollution, 2007

1. Los Angeles–Long Beach–Riverside, California
2. Pittsburgh–New Castle, Pennsylvania
3. Bakersfield, California
4. Birmingham-Hoover–Cullman, Alabama
5. Detroit–Warren–Flint, Michigan
6. Cleveland–Akron–Elyria, Ohio
7. Visalia–Porterville, California
8. Cincinnati, Ohio; Middletown, Kentucky; Wilmington, Indiana
9. Indianapolis–Anderson–Columbus, Indiana
10. St. Louis–St. Charles, Missouri

Source: American Lung Association (by year-round particle pollution)

the industrial process that cause pollution. They also might recommend air pollution control equipment or advise the manufacturer to use different raw materials or machinery.

Some engineers work as independent consultants. They advise businesses about how to operate in order to limit air pollution. Other air quality engineers work for equipment manufacturers that design and sell air pollution control systems.

Some air quality engineers work for the U.S. Environmental Protection Agency (EPA) and other governmental agencies that decide how much of certain chemicals are harmful. They investigate manufacturers that may be polluters and may even go to court to force manufacturers to comply with the law.

Some air quality engineers research the causes and effects of specific problems such as sick building syndrome, acid rain, or the greenhouse effect.

Did You Know?

○ Forty-six percent of the U.S. population lives in counties that have unhealthful levels of either particle pollution or ozone (a highly reactive gas that can be unhealthy to humans).
○ More than one-third of the U.S. population resides in areas with unhealthful levels of ozone—a decrease of 17 percent from 2006.
○ Approximately 38.3 million Americans live in 32 counties that have unhealthful levels of all three types of air pollutants: ozone, short-term particle pollution, and year-round particle pollution.

Source: *State of the Air: 2007*, American Lung Association

Air quality engineers are committed to research and development and work in public or private research institutions and in academic environments.

Education and Training

High school classes in math, biology, and chemistry will be helpful if you are interested in becoming an air quality engineer.

You will also need a bachelor's degree in environmental or chemical engineering to work in this career. College programs will cover specific concerns of air quality engineers, such as how pollution affects health and how weather and air pollution interact. In addition, knowledge of advanced computer systems is becoming more and more important in the field of engineering.

EXPLORING

○ Learning about air pollution problems such as the greenhouse effect and acid rain will help you understand what sorts of challenges air quality engineers will face in the years to come. Visit http://epa.gov/climatechange/kids/greenhouse.html to learn more about the greenhouse effect and http://www.epa.gov/acidrain to learn more about acid rain.

○ Contact a local branch of the EPA to find out about air pollution control issues in your area.

○ Ask your science teacher to set up a presentation by an air quality engineer.

Earnings

Salaries for entry-level engineers start at around $30,000 to $35,000 per year. Local government agencies pay at the lower end of the scale; state and federal agencies, slightly higher. Salaries in the private sector are highest, from $40,000 up to $70,000 or more.

Outlook

Air quality management has a bright future. Most people are understandably concerned about the quality of the air they breathe. As a result, the public exerts pressure on the government to control pollution emissions. Most industries will need engineers to determine how they can control their own pollutants. As manufacturing processes develop and change, industries will need air quality engineers to monitor their new technologies.

Job opportunities will probably be better in areas of the country targeted by the EPA (generally larger cities, such as Los Angeles, Chicago, and Denver).

FOR MORE INFO

For information on careers and a list of colleges and degrees offering environmental degrees, contact
Air and Waste Management Association
420 Fort Duquesne Boulevard
One Gateway Center, Third Floor
Pittsburgh, PA 15222-1435
Tel: 412-232-3444
E-mail: info@awma.org
http://www.awma.org

For information on careers, contact
Junior Engineering Technical Society
1420 King Street, Suite 405
Alexandria, VA 22314-2750
Tel: 703-548-5387
E-mail: info@jets.org
http://www.jets.org

For information on air pollution and government pollution control boards, contact
National Association of Clean Air Agencies
444 North Capitol Street NW, Suite 307
Washington, DC 20001-1512
Tel: 202-624-7864
E-mail: 4clnair@4cleanair.org
http://www.cleanairworld.org

For information about air quality and other environmental issues, contact
U.S. Environmental Protection Agency
Ariel Rios Building
1200 Pennsylvania Avenue NW
Washington, DC 20460
Tel: 202-260-2090
http://www.epa.gov

Ecologists

What Ecologists Do

Ecologists study how plants and animals interact and sustain each other in their environments. An environment not only includes living things, but also nonliving elements, such as chemicals, moisture, soil, light, temperature, and man-made things, such as buildings, highways, machines, fertilizers, and medicines. The word ecology is sometimes used to describe the balance of nature.

Much of ecologists' work involves the study of communities. A community is the group of organisms that share a particular habitat, or environment. For example, a *forest ecologist* might

Words to Learn

canopy the upper layer of a forest, created by the foliage and branches of the tallest trees

coniferous trees that bear cones

ecosystem a community of animals and plants and their interaction with the nonliving environment

effluent wastewater or sewage that flows into a river, lake, or ocean

riparian zone forest or grass growing on the banks of a stream; the riparian zone can prevent soil erosion

savanna a flat, grassy plain found in tropical areas

tundra a cold region where the soil under the surface of the ground is permanently frozen

watershed the gathering ground of a river system, a ridge that separates two river basins, or an area of land that slopes into a river or lake

EXPLORING

○ Read books and other publications about ecology and the environment.

○ Join a scouting organization or environmental protection group to gain firsthand experience in the work of an ecologist.

○ Visit natural history museums to learn more about the field. Visit nearby parks or forest preserves.

○ Talk to an ecologist about his or her career. Ask the following questions: What made you want to become an ecologist? What do you like most and least about your job? How did you train to become an ecologist? What advice would you give to someone interested in the career?

research how changes in the environment affect forests.

Some ecologists study biomes, which are large communities. Examples of biomes are the tropical rain forest, the prairie, the tundra, and the desert. The ocean is sometimes considered as one biome.

Many ecologists focus their studies on the ecosystem—a community together with its nonliving components. *Population ecologists* study why a certain population of living things increases, decreases, or remains stable.

Since all living things, including humans, are dependent on their environments, the work of ecologists is extremely important in helping us understand how the environment works. The study of ecology helps protect, clean, improve, and preserve our environment. Ecologists investigate industry and government actions and help correct past environmental problems.

Education and Training

High school classes that will be especially useful include earth science, biology, chemistry, English, and math.

To be an ecologist you must go to college and earn a bachelor's degree. Recommended majors are biology, botany, chemistry, ecology, geology, physics, or zoology.

You will need a master's degree for research or management jobs. For higher positions, such as college teacher or research supervisor, you'll need a doctoral degree.

Ecological Catastrophe

An example of an ecological catastrophe occurred in Borneo shortly after World War II (1939–1945). A program was undertaken there to control mosquitoes by spraying DDT, an insecticide. The number of mosquitoes declined drastically, but the roofs of houses began to collapse because caterpillars were eating them. The caterpillar population had previously been held under control by certain predatory wasps—which also had been killed off by the DDT.

In addition to spraying for mosquitoes, the villagers also sprayed inside their homes to kill flies. Previously, geckos (a type of lizard) had reduced the housefly population. When the geckos ate the DDT-laden houseflies, however, they began to die. Then the house cats that had eaten the dead or dying geckos began to die from the DDT concentrated in the bodies. So many cats died that rats began invading the houses, eating the villagers' food. The rats multiplied and eventually became potential plague carriers.

Earnings

Salaries for ecologists vary depending on such factors as their level of education, experience, area of specialization, and the organization for which they work. The U.S. Department of Labor reported the median annual income of environmental scientists and specialists as $56,100 in 2006. Salaries ranged from less than $34,590 to $94,670 or more annually.

The Evolution of Ecology

The term "ecology" was first defined in 1866 by Ernst Haeckel (1834–1919), a German biologist. Haeckel was fascinated with the links between living things and their physical environment. Recognizing that there was such a link was a key step in the development of the science of ecology.

Outlook

The job outlook for environmental workers in general should remain good in the next decade. But there will be fewer jobs in land and water conservation. This is because so many ecologists compete for these popular jobs. Also, many environmental organizations have tight budgets that keep them from hiring large numbers of ecologists.

FOR MORE INFO

For a wide variety of publications, including Issues in Ecology, Careers in Ecology, *and fact sheets about specific ecological concerns, contact*
Ecological Society of America
1707 H Street NW, Suite 400
Washington, DC 20006-3919
Tel: 202-833-8773
E-mail: esahq@esa.org
http://esa.org

For information on paid internships and careers in the field, contact
Environmental Careers Organization

30 Winter Street, Sixth Floor
Boston, MA 02108
Tel: 617-426-4783
http://www.eco.org

For information on student volunteer activities and programs, contact
Student Conservation Association
689 River Road
PO Box 550
Charlestown, NH 03603-0550
Tel: 603-543-1700
E-mail: ask-us@sca-inc.org
http://www.thesca.org

Energy Conservation Technicians

What Energy Conservation Technicians Do

Energy conservation technicians study how machines use energy and develop ways to use that energy more effectively. Working under the supervision of engineers or other professionals, they conduct research, perform tests, and repair or replace machines. Technicians work in a wide variety of locations, including nuclear power plants, research laboratories, and construction companies.

Conserving Energy at Home

○ Dress appropriately in the house to help reduce heating and cooling costs.

○ Turn off lights and appliances when they are not in use.

○ Try to run your dishwasher or washing machine only when you have a full load to clean. Use cold water in the washing machine, when possible. Air-dry dishes and laundry.

○ Replace regular lightbulbs with compact fluorescent lights, which use about one-fourth of the energy of regular lightbulbs.

○ Ride your bike or walk to school and to other activities to save gas and reduce pollution.

○ Plant leafy trees near your home. They lose their leaves in the fall and allow the sun in to help heat your home during the winter. During the summer, the leaves cool the house by blocking the sun.

○ Recycle plastics, glass, steel and aluminum cans, and newspapers.

○ Purchase products that are made of recycled material.

Sources: U.S. Department of Energy, Earth 911

EXPLORING

○ Read about energy conservation techniques in books and on the Internet.

○ Contact employers of energy technicians to learn about opportunities for volunteer, part-time, or summer work. Major employers of energy conservation technicians include utility companies, large hospitals, office buildings, hotels, colleges and universities, and manufacturing plants.

There are four areas in which energy conservation technicians work: energy research and development, energy production, energy use, and energy conservation.

Those in research and development design, build, and operate new laboratory experiments for physicists, chemists, or engineers. Technicians in energy production often work for power plants. In the field of energy use, a technician might be hired to make heavy industrial equipment work more efficiently. A technician involved in energy conservation might study how a building could use energy more efficiently.

After running tests and measurements, the technician usually prepares a report and discusses the results with management officials. Then, technicians may make recommendations, but managers make the final decisions about what actions should be taken. After a final decision is made, technicians team up with other workers to see that any necessary corrections are done.

Education and Training

The best way to enter this career is to complete a two-year training program at a community college or technical school. The program might be called energy conservation technology, electric power maintenance, or general engineering technology. To be accepted into such a program, you should be a high school graduate with course work in mathematics, physics, and chemistry. Other helpful courses are ecology, computer science, and mechanical or architectural drafting.

To Be a Successful Energy Conservation Technician, You Should . . .

○ have a solid background in how machines operate

○ be able to read blueprints and sketches

○ be able to follow instructions from supervisors

○ be good at mathematics and the physical sciences

○ have the ability to describe problems in technical language for engineers and in clear terms for people outside the profession

Earnings

Earnings of energy conservation technicians vary greatly based on the amount of formal training and experience they have. According to the U.S. Department of Labor, the mean annual salary for environmental engineering technicians in engineering and architectural services (a category that often includes energy conservation technicians) was $40,540 in 2006. Salaries for all environmental engineering technicians ranged from less than $25,110 to $66,120 or more annually.

Outlook

Since energy use constitutes a major expense, the demand for energy conservation technicians is likely to remain strong.

FOR MORE INFO

For industry information, contact
Association of Energy Engineers
4025 Pleasantdale Road, Suite 420
Atlanta, GA 30340-4260
Tel: 770-447-5083
http://www.aeecenter.org

For information on energy efficiency and renewable energy, contact
Energy Efficiency and Renewable Energy
U.S. Department of Energy
Mail Stop EE-1
Washington, DC 20585
http://www.eere.energy.gov

Utility companies, manufacturers, and government agencies are working together to establish energy efficiency standards. They are developing programs to improve energy efficiency in commercial air-conditioning equipment, lighting, geothermal heat pumps, and other systems. Programs such as these will create job opportunities for technicians.

Environmental Engineers

What Environmental Engineers Do

If a private company or a municipality does not handle its waste streams properly, it can face thousands or even millions of dollars in fines for breaking the law. A waste stream can be anything from wastewater, to solid waste (garbage), to hazardous waste (such as radioactive waste), to air pollution. *Environmental engineers* play an important role in controlling waste streams.

Environmental engineers may plan a sewage system, design a manufacturing plant's emissions system, or develop a plan for a landfill site needed to bury garbage. Scientists help decide how

Words to Learn

biodegradation the use of bacteria or other living organisms to decompose contaminants

CERCLA (Comprehensive Environmental Response, Compensation, and Liability Act) a 1980 law (known as "Superfund") that mandated cleanup of private and government-owned hazardous waste sites

EPA (U.S. Environmental Protection Agency) the federal agency responsible for overseeing the implementation of environmental laws, including those designed to monitor and control air, water, and soil pollution; state EPAs help carry out these laws

hazardous waste any discarded substance, usually chemicals, that can cause harm to humans

National Priorities List U.S. EPA list of the worst hazardous waste sites in the country needing cleanup

remediation environmental cleanup

septic anaerobic (without air) decomposition typically accompanied by an unpleasant odor

EXPLORING

○ Surf the Web and check your library and bookstore for reading material on engineering and the environment. *Chemical & Engineering News* (http://pubs.acs.org/cen) regularly features articles on waste management systems.

○ Volunteer for the local chapter of a nonprofit environmental organization.

○ Talk to an environmental engineer about his or her career. Contact your local EPA office, check the Yellow Pages for environmental consulting firms in your area, or ask a local industrial company if you can visit.

to break down the waste, but engineers figure out how the system will be built and how it will work.

Environmental engineers may work for private industrial companies, for the Environmental Protection Agency (EPA), or for engineering consulting firms. Environmental engineers who work for private industrial companies help make sure their companies obey environmental laws. That may mean designing new waste systems or making sure the old ones are operating up to standard.

Environmental engineers who work for the EPA might not design the waste treatment systems themselves, but they do have to know how such systems are designed and built. If there is a pollution problem in their area, they need to figure out if a waste control system is causing the problem, and what might have gone wrong.

Environmental engineers employed by engineering consulting firms work on many different types of problems. They design and build waste control systems for their clients. They also deal with the EPA on behalf of their clients, filling out forms and checking to see what requirements must be met.

Education and Training

In high school, take as much science and mathematics as possible. You will have to earn a bachelor's degree to work as an environmental engineer. About 20 colleges offer a bachelor's degree in environmental engineering. Another option is to earn another type of engineering degree such as civil, industrial, or mechanical engineering, with additional courses in environmental engineering.

Earnings

The U.S. Department of Labor reports that median annual earnings of environmental engineers were $69,940 in 2006. Salaries ranged from less than $43,180 to more than $106,230.

Outlook

The *Occupational Outlook Handbook* predicts that employment for environmental engineers will grow much faster than average. Engineers will be needed to clean up existing hazards and help companies comply with government regulations. The shift toward preventing problems and protecting public health should create job opportunities.

An environmental engineer pours a sample of water he has taken from the Hudson River in New York. His engineering firm is monitoring the level of PCBs, an environmental pollutant, in the water. (David M. Jennings, The Image Works)

FOR MORE INFO

For information on careers, contact
American Academy of Environmental Engineers
130 Holiday Court, Suite 100
Annapolis, MD 21401-7003
Tel: 410-266-3311
E-mail: info@aaee.net
http://www.aaee.net

For information on student volunteer activities and programs, contact
Student Conservation Association
689 River Road
PO Box 550
Charlestown, NH 03603-0550
Tel: 603-543-1700
E-mail: ask-us@sca-inc.org
http://www.thesca.org

Environmental Lobbyists

What Environmental Lobbyists Do

Lobbyists try to persuade legislators and other public office holders, as well as the general public, to support the interests of their clients. *Environmental lobbyists* are lobbyists who deal specifically with environmental issues. There is a huge range of environmental issues that are brought before local, state, and federal governments every year. Clean air, soil, and water; global climate change; genetic modification of crops; renewable energy; wildlife preservation; and conservation of natural resources are just a few of the major issues.

Environmental lobbyists try to influence legislators and government officials through both direct and indirect lobbying. Direct lobbying involves reaching legislators themselves. Environmental lobbyists meet with members of Congress, their staff members, and other members of government. They call government officials to discuss the impact various measures might have on the environment. They sometimes testify before congressional committees or state legislatures. They distribute letters and fact sheets to legislators' offices. They may try to approach legislators as they travel to and from their offices, or they could ask legislators who share their views to broach issues with other, less sympathetic legislators. They might also try to persuade members of Congress to serve as cosponsors of bills the lobbyists support. When a member of Congress becomes a cosponsor of a bill, his or her name is added to the list of members supporting that measure. Lobbyists typically assume that cosponsors will vote to support the bill. A bill's chances of one day becoming a law dramatically improve as more members agree to serve as cosponsors.

Indirect lobbying, also called grassroots lobbying, involves educating and motivating the public. The goal of indirect lobbying is to encourage the public to urge their representatives to vote for or against certain legislation. Environmental lobbyists use a wide variety of indirect techniques. They issue press releases about pending legislation, hoping to inspire members of the media to write topical articles. They mail letters to citizens, urging them to write or call their representatives. They post information on the Internet and sometimes go door-to-door with information to mobilize the public to become members of environmental groups. On rare occasions, they take concerned citizens to state capitals or to Washington, D.C., to meet with representatives.

Lobbyists must register with government authorities and submit reports on the money they collect and spend during lobbying activities.

EXPLORING

- ○ Get involved in school government. Serve on the student council or work on student election campaigns.
- ○ Volunteer with an environmental organization.
- ○ Write for your school or community newspaper. Try to write stories about environmental issues affecting your school or community.
- ○ Work on publicity and advertising for school and community organizations and events.
- ○ Join the debate team or work for the school radio station to help you develop your communication and research skills.

Education and Training

If you are interested in a career as an environmental lobbyist, classes in speech and communications are important, and political science and journalism classes are helpful as well. You also should take biology, ecology, environmental science, and

To Be a Successful Environmental Lobbyist, You Should . . .

○ be committed to protecting the environment

○ have excellent communication skills

○ be able to work well in teams

○ be able to perform well under pressure

○ have a good understanding of the political process

○ be confident and outgoing

chemistry in order to learn about the scientific issues behind environmental legislation.

Lobbyists have undergraduate degrees in political science, journalism, or public relations. They often hold graduate degrees in law or political science, as well. Most lobbyists enter the career after gaining a great deal of experience in another government career, such as with Congress as a legislative aide, or as a press secretary.

Earnings

A lobbyist's income depends on the size of the organization he or she represents. Experienced lobbyists with a solid client base can earn well over $100,000 a year, and some make more than $500,000 a year. Beginning lobbyists may make less than $20,000 a year as they build a client base.

Outlook

There is no shortage of environmental concerns in our country. As long as people continue to pollute our air, water, and soil, cut down forests, develop land, and mine the Earth, environmental

Lobbyists Gain Respect

In the late 1700s, the term *lobbyist* was used to describe the special-interest representatives who gathered in the anteroom, or lobby, outside the legislative chamber in the New York State Capitol. In the 20th century, lobbyists came to be considered as experts in the fields that they represented. Members of Congress relied on them to provide information needed to evaluate legislation.

In 1946, the Federal Regulation of Lobbying Act was passed into law. The act requires that anyone who spends or receives money or anything of value in the interests of passing, modifying, or defeating legislation be registered and provide spending reports. Most recently, the Lobbying Disclosure Act of 1995 requires all lobbyists working at the federal level to be registered.

groups will continue to fight for legislation that will protect our natural resources. This profession is, therefore, expected to grow about as fast as the average through the next decade.

FOR MORE INFO

For additional information about a career as a lobbyist, contact
American League of Lobbyists
PO Box 30005
Alexandria, VA 22310-8005
Tel: 703-960-3011
http://www.alldc.org

For information on paid internships and careers in the field, contact
Environmental Careers Organization
30 Winter Street, Sixth Floor
Boston, MA 02108
Tel: 617-426-4783
http://www.eco.org

Environmental Technicians

What Environmental Technicians Do

Environmental technicians test water, air, and soil for contamination by pollutants. Most environmental technicians specialize in one type of pollution. Environmental technicians are sometimes called *pollution control technicians.*

Water pollution technicians collect samples from bodies of water or from wastewater. They perform chemical tests that show if it is contaminated or polluted. In addition to testing the water, technicians may set up equipment to monitor water over a period of time to see if it is becoming polluted.

Air pollution technicians collect and analyze samples of gas emissions and the atmosphere. They often set up monitoring equipment outdoors to take air samples or they may try to create the same conditions in a laboratory.

Soil technicians or *land pollution technicians* collect soil, silt, or mud samples so they can be checked for contamination. Soil can be contaminated when polluted water or waste seeps into the earth.

Noise pollution technicians use rooftop devices and mobile units to check noise levels of factories, highways, airports, and other locations. High noise levels can harm workers or the public.

Pollution Solution

One creative solution to control pollution is phytoremediation. Phytoremediation is the use of plants and trees to clean up contaminated soil and water. Plants can break down organic pollutants or stabilize metal contaminants by acting as filters or traps. Over time, plants soak up contaminants from the soil or water into their root systems.

In the eastern United States, where acid mine drainage is a problem, the Department of the Interior encourages the planting of wetlands using the common cattail to soak up mining contaminants from streams.

Education and Training

Pollution control is highly technical work, so you should take as many mathematics and laboratory science courses as possible in high school. Communications, computer science, conservation, and ecology studies are also important.

After high school, you need to complete a two-year program in environmental technology. These programs are offered at community and junior colleges, and at technical schools. Some employers also offer on-the-job training for new employees.

Earnings

According to the U.S. Department of Labor, the average annual salary for environmental science and protection technicians was $38,090 in 2006.

EXPLORING

○ Read technical and general-interest publications about environmental science and pollution control.

○ Join a nature or environmental science club to learn about general issues in the field.

○ Visit a municipal health department or pollution control agency in your community. Many agencies are pleased to explain their work to visitors.

○ Tour a local manufacturing plant that uses air- or water-pollution abatement systems.

It's the Law!

Environmental laws passed in the 1960s and later created the need for professionals to monitor and regulate pollution of soil, water, and air. Three of the most important environmental laws are the Clean Air Act, the Clean Water Act, and the Pollution Prevention Act.

The Clean Air Act (1970) regulates air emissions from factories and other sources. The act sets maximum pollutant standards.

The Clean Water Act (1972) strives to protect healthy waters and to restore polluted ones.

The Pollution Prevention Act (1990) encourages industry, government, and the public to reduce pollution by making better use of raw materials.

An environmental technician conducts a test that will determine the level of pollutants in water runoff from farms near a new housing development. (Peggy Greb, USDA, Agricultural Research Service)

Salaries ranged from less than $23,600 to more than $60,700. Technicians who worked for local government earned mean annual salaries of $43,050 in 2006. Those who were employed by state governments earned $43,810. Technicians who become managers or supervisors can earn $70,000 per year or more.

Outlook

Demand for environmental technicians should continue at an average pace in the next decade. Those trained to handle complex technical demands will find the best jobs. As long as the federal government supports pollution control, the environmental control industry will continue to grow.

FOR MORE INFO

For information on careers and a list of colleges and degrees offering environmental degrees, contact
Air and Waste Management Association
420 Fort Duquesne Boulevard
One Gateway Center, Third Floor
Pittsburgh, PA 15222-1435
Tel: 412-232-3444
E-mail: info@awma.org
http://www.awma.org

The following organization is an environmental careers resource for high school and college students.

Environmental Careers Organization
30 Winter Street, Sixth Floor
Boston, MA 02108
Tel: 617-426-4783
http://www.eco.org

For information on environmental careers and student employment opportunities, contact
U.S. Environmental Protection Agency
Ariel Rios Building
1200 Pennsylvania Avenue NW
Washington, DC 20460-0001
Tel: 202-260-2090
http://www.epa.gov

Foresters

What Foresters Do

Foresters protect and manage forests. They identify areas that need care, which may include planting trees, controlling diseases or insects, scattering seeds, or pruning trees. They map the locations of resources, such as timber, game shelter, food, snow, and water. Foresters lay out logging roads or roads to lakes and campgrounds. Some foresters create the plans for building campgrounds and shelters, supervise crews, and inspect the work after it is done.

Foresters select and mark trees to be cut. They are in charge of the lookouts, patrols, and pilots who watch for fires. They also lead crews that fight fires. Some foresters supervise campgrounds, find lost hikers, and rescue climbers and skiers.

Foresters must record the work done in the forest on maps and in reports. Sometimes they use computers and data processing equipment. They also use aerial photography. Some foresters work in the laboratories and factories of wood-related industries, such as sawmills, pulp and paper mills, wood preserving plants, and furniture factories. Others do research in laboratories, greenhouses, and forests.

Foresters may specialize. For example, *silviculturists* specialize in the establishment and reproduction of forests. They regulate forest makeup, and manage forest growth and development. *Forest engineers* design and construct roads, bridges, dams, and buildings in forest

Did You Know?

Approximately 32,000 foresters and conservation scientists are employed in the United States, according to the U.S. Department of Labor. About two-thirds of U.S. foresters are employed by government agencies, such as the Forest Service, the Bureau of Land Management, and the National Park Service, as well as state and local agencies.

EXPLORING

○ Visit the Web sites of colleges and universities that offer programs in forestry. Consult http://www.safnet.org for a list of programs.
○ Visit local forest preserves. Most preserves offer education programs and workshops. Some may have volunteer programs.
○ In some parts of the country, local chapters of the Society of American Foresters invite prospective forestry students to some of their meetings and field trips.
○ Talk with someone already working as a forester or forestry technician. Your science teacher or guidance counselor may be able to help you arrange a meeting.

areas. These construction projects help the movement of logs and pulpwood out of the forest. *Forest ecologists* conduct research to determine how forests are affected by changes in environmental conditions, such as light, soil, climate, altitude, and animals.

Education and Training

To prepare for this field, take as many mathematics and sciences courses as possible in high school. Take algebra, geometry, and statistics as well as biology, chemistry, physics, and any science course that will teach you about ecology and forestry. English classes are also important since part of your job is likely to include researching, writing reports, and presenting your findings. In addition, take history, economics, and, if possible, agriculture classes, which will teach you about soils and plant growth, among other things.

A professional forester must graduate from a four-year school of forestry with a bachelor's degree. Some foresters have master's degrees. Most schools of forestry are part of state universities. In forestry school, you learn how to tend and reproduce forests. In addition, you study forest economics and the harvesting and marketing of forest crops. You work in the forest as a part of your university training.

Earnings

According to the U.S. Department of Labor, median annual earnings of foresters were $51,190 in 2006. Salaries ranged from less than $33,490 to more than $74,570.

In 2005, most bachelor's degree graduates entering federal government jobs as foresters, range managers, or soil conservationists earned $24,677 or $30,567, depending on college records. Those with master's degrees earned $37,390 or $45,239 to start, and those with doctorates started at $54,221. In 2006, foresters employed by the federal government earned mean salaries of $57,280.

A forester prunes an evergreen tree. (Gaetano, Corbis)

Outlook

Job opportunities in forestry are expected to grow more slowly than the average due to budget cuts that have limited hiring new workers. Also, federal land management agencies, such as the Forest Service, are giving less attention to timber programs and are focusing more on conserving wildlife, promoting recreation, and sustaining ecosystems.

A Better Way to Plant

Foresters and woodland owners often renew harvested forest areas by planting seeds or seedlings of particular kinds of trees. These seedlings are usually grown in large nurseries and transplanted when they are hardy and old enough to survive.

When companies first began replanting harvested forests, all of the planting was done by hand. Since the 1940s, however, tree-planting machines have done more and more of the replanting. As the planting machine is pulled behind a tractor, a plowlike blade cuts open a furrow in the ground. A forestry worker places the seedlings in the ground by hand. Wheels on the planting machine close the furrow around the seedling. Machine planting allows a crew to plant thousands of seedlings in one day.

Forest Facts

○ Most forest fires are now detected by aircraft or closed-circuit television, rather than by traditional lookout towers.

○ There are 747 million acres of forestland in the United States.

○ The largest forest area in the United States is the Central Hardwood Forest, which stretches across eastern North America and encompasses part or all of 28 U.S. states and two Canadian provinces.

○ Older, slower-growing trees and trees that have been damaged by fire or drought are most vulnerable to attack by disease and insects.

Cutbacks in timber harvesting on public lands, most of which are located in the Northwest and California, have also slowed job growth for private industry foresters. Opportunities will be better for foresters on privately owned land in the Southeast. Landowners and industries, such as paper companies, sawmills, and pulpwood mills, will continue to need foresters.

FOR MORE INFO

For information on forestry and forests in the United States, contact

American Forests
PO Box 2000
Washington, DC 20013-2000
Tel: 202-737-1944
E-mail: info@amfor.org
http://www.americanforests.org

For information on forestry careers and schools, contact

Society of American Foresters
5400 Grosvenor Lane

Bethesda, MD 20814-2198
Tel: 866-897-8720
E-mail: safweb@safnet.org
http://www.safnet.org

For information about government careers in forestry and facts about national forests across the country, contact

USDA Forest Service
1400 Independence Avenue SW
Washington, DC 20250-0003
Tel: 202-205-8333
http://www.fs.fed.us

Geologists

What Geologists Do

Geologists study the Earth—how it was formed, what it is made of, and how it is slowly changing. They study rock samples in their laboratories under controlled temperatures and pressures. Finally, they organize the information they have gathered and write reports. These reports may be used to locate groundwater, oil, minerals, and other natural resources.

Many geologists specialize in a particular study of the Earth. For example, those who study the oceans are called *marine geologists*. Those who try to locate natural gas and oil deposits are called *petroleum geologists*. *Paleontologists* study the Earth's rock formations to determine the age of the Earth. *Engineering geologists* are responsible for the application of geological knowledge to problems that arise in the construction of roads, buildings, bridges, dams, and other structures. *Petrologists* study the origin and composition of igneous, metamorphic, and sedimentary rocks. *Stratigraphers* study the distribution and relative arrangement of sedimentary rock layers. *Geohydrologists* study the nature and distribution of water within the Earth. They are often involved in environmental impact studies. *Geomorphologists* study the form of the Earth's surface and the processes, such as erosion and glaciation, that bring about changes.

Major Employers of Geologists

- oil and gas companies and other private businesses
- federal government, including the Department of the Interior (the U.S. Geological Survey and the Bureau of Reclamation) and the Departments of Defense, Agriculture, and Commerce
- state and local government agencies
- research organizations
- colleges and universities
- museums

EXPLORING

○ Try to read as much as possible about geology and geologists. Here are some reading suggestions: *Geology Crafts For Kids: 50 Nifty Projects to Explore the Marvels of Planet Earth,* by Alan Anderson, Gwen Diehn, and Terry Krautwurst (Sterling, 1998); *Geology Rocks!: 50 Hands-On Activities to Explore the Earth,* by Cindy Blobaum and Michael Kline (Williamson, 1999); and *The Practical Encyclopedia of Rocks & Minerals,* by John Farndon (Lorenz Books, 2006).

○ Amateur geological groups and local museums may have geology clubs you can join.

○ Ask your science teacher or guidance counselor to arrange an information interview with a geologist.

Geologists' work can be physically demanding. They travel often to remote and rugged sites by helicopter or four-wheel-drive vehicle and cover large areas on foot. In addition, they spend long hours working in the laboratory and preparing reports.

Education and Training

Take computer science, history, English, and geography classes while in high school. Science and math classes are also important to take, particularly earth science, chemistry, and physics. Math classes should include algebra, trigonometry, and statistics.

To be a geologist, you need to earn a bachelor's degree, usually in geology, or in the physical and earth sciences. Positions in research, teaching, or exploration require a master's degree. Geologists who want to teach at a college or university or head a department in a commercial business must earn a doctorate.

Earnings

The U.S. Department of Labor reports that the median annual salary for geoscientists was $72,660 in 2006. Salaries ranged from less $39,740 to more than $135,950 a year. In the federal government, the average salary for geologists was $86,240 a year in 2006.

What Do Geological Technicians Do?

Geological technicians help geologists study the Earth's physical makeup and history. This includes the exploration of mountain uplifting, rock formations, mineral deposits, earthquakes, and volcanoes.

Geological technicians most often work as part of a research team. Most often, geological technicians work with petroleum geologists. These scientists determine where deposits of oil and natural gas may be buried beneath the Earth's surface. Geological technicians draw maps to show where drilling operations are taking place. They write reports that geologists use to determine where an oil deposit might be located.

Geological technicians also draw maps that show exactly where a drilling crew has dug a well. The map tells whether or not oil was found and specifies the depth of the well.

Some geological technicians work in the field of environmental engineering. They help geologists study how structures, such as roads, landfills, and buildings, affect the environment.

Outlook

The U.S. Department of Labor predicts that employment of geologists will grow more slowly than the average. Geologists will find jobs in the petroleum industry, but competition for those jobs will be strong. Many of these positions may be

Rock-Collecting Tips

Many people collect rocks as a hobby. Some gather them for color, such as agate with its bands of many hues. Others collect specimens for odd or beautiful shapes. Some look for imprints of fossils.

For people who want to do their own collecting, every part of the country offers specimens. Mountains, seashores, riverbanks, woods, and lava plains are especially abundant in varied rocks. Many people simply pick up rocks on the surface of the ground. Others carry rock hammers, picks, and Geiger counters (a device that detects radiation). Hobbyists can buy rocks from specialty stores or scientific supply houses.

in foreign countries. Geologists may also find jobs in environmental protection and reclamation (cleanup). Those with master's degrees and those familiar with computer modeling and the Global Positioning System will have the best employment opportunities.

FOR MORE INFO

For information on careers, contact
American Geological Institute
4220 King Street
Alexandria, VA 22302-1502
Tel: 703-379-2480
http://www.agiweb.org

American Institute of Professional Geologists
1400 West 122nd Avenue, Suite 250
Westminster, CO 80234-3499
Tel: 303-412-6205
E-mail: aipg@aipg.org
http://www.aipg.org

Geological Society of America
PO Box 9140
Boulder, CO 80301-9140
Tel: 888-443-4472
E-mail: gsaservice@geosociety.org
http://www.geosociety.org

For career and educational information about the geosciences, visit
U.S. Geological Survey
http://education.usgs.gov

For information on student chapters, contact
Association of Environmental & Engineering Geologists
PO Box 460518
Denver, CO 80246-0518
Tel: 303-757-2926
E-mail: aeg@aegweb.org
http://aegweb.org

Groundwater Professionals

What Groundwater Professionals Do

In addition to the water you see at the surface of the Earth, there is water under the ground, known as groundwater. This includes underground streams and aquifers, which are layers of water-bearing rock or sand. *Groundwater professionals* monitor groundwater quality, map groundwater supplies, and find ways to clean up contaminated groundwater. They also find new sources of quality groundwater, bring it to the surface, and make sure that it is managed properly.

Groundwater professionals include all scientists and other workers concerned with groundwater. For example, some *geologists* help a local water district locate a new source of groundwater. *Civil engineers* design the wells and pumps needed to get the water to the surface, and *hydrogeologists* and *chemists* test the water to make sure it is safe to drink. Groundwater professionals use the scientific principles of geology, chemistry, mathematics, engineering, and physics in their work.

Some groundwater professionals gather information on the quality of water to ensure that it is safe to use. They test water samples for signs of pollution. They must be aware of chemicals or garbage that could drain into the water supply from a waste disposal site or other location.

Education and Training

To become a groundwater professional, you should have a solid background in mathematics and science, particularly the

To Be a Successful Groundwater Professional, You Should . . .

○ be curious and able to solve complex problems

○ have good communication skills

○ be attentive to detail

○ be able to work as part of a team

○ have a complete understanding of the many governmental rules and regulations concerning groundwater

physical and earth sciences. Technology is important in this field, so make sure you have computer skills.

You will need to earn a bachelor's degree to begin a career as a groundwater professional. Geology, civil engineering, and chemistry are common undergraduate majors in this field. Engineering, geology, hydrogeology (the science of groundwater supplies), hydrology (the study of water and its properties), geophysics, petroleum geology, mining, engineering, or other related degrees also are useful. Many people in this field also have a master's or a doctoral degree.

Earnings

Earnings for groundwater professionals vary greatly depending on the type of work they do, training and experience required for the work, geographic region, type of employer, and other factors.

EXPLORING

○ Visit the Web sites of professional groundwater associations (see "For More Info").

○ Volunteer for a nonprofit environmental organization to gain experience in the field.

○ Ask at a landfill, consulting firm, government agency, or local water district if they are willing to give tours (so you can see groundwater professionals in action) or answer questions.

Groundwater professionals earn salaries in the upper range of those for all water industry professionals. The U.S. Department of Labor reports that hydrologists earned median annual salaries of $66,260 in 2006. The lowest 10 percent earned less than $42,080, and the highest 10 percent earned $98,320 or more.

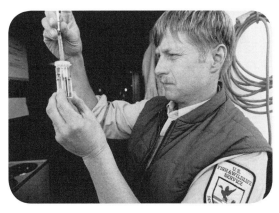

A U.S. Fish & Wildlife Service biologist checks oxygen and carbon dioxide levels in a water sample. (Jim West, The Image Works)

Outlook

The *Occupational Outlook Handbook* predicts that employment for hydrologists and environmental scientists will grow much faster than the average. Amendments to the Resource Conservation and Recovery Act, the Clean Water Act, and other legislation signal that groundwater is a priority to the government. Private industry needs to obey stricter regulations, including those related to keeping groundwater safe from contamination. Local, regional, and state authorities need to map, develop, and protect their groundwater supplies. Consultants need the specific expertise that groundwater professionals can offer. Research is needed to develop new ways to treat contaminated groundwater, to prevent spills and leaks, and to

Did You Know?

○ There are nearly 170,000 public water systems in the United States.

○ Freshwater makes up only 2.5 percent of all water on the Earth. Most of this water is frozen at the Earth's poles.

○ More than 1.1 billion people worldwide do not have access to a safe and adequate water supply.

Sources: Environmental Protection Agency, WaterPartners International, American Water Works Association

develop systems that will make the most of groundwater supplies. All of this will result in work opportunities for groundwater professionals in the near future.

FOR MORE INFO

For information on the hydrologic sciences, contact
American Geophysical Union
2000 Florida Avenue NW
Washington, DC 20009-1277
Tel: 800-966-2481
E-mail: service@agu.org
http://www.agu.org

For information on student chapters and related organizations, contact
American Institute of Hydrology
300 Village Green Circle, Suite 201
Smyrna, GA 30080-3451
Tel: 770-384-1634
E-mail: aihydro@aol.com
http://www.aihydro.org

For information on water quality and supply, contact
American Water Works Association
6666 West Quincy Avenue
Denver, CO 80235-3098
Tel: 800-926-7337
http://www.awwa.org

National Ground Water Association
601 Dempsey Road
Westerville, OH 43081-8978
Tel: 800-551-7379
E-mail: ngwa@ngwa.org
http://www.ngwa.org

U.S. Environmental Protection Agency
Office of Ground Water and Drinking Water
http://www.epa.gov/safewater

Hazardous Waste Management Specialists

What Hazardous Waste Management Specialists Do

Hazardous materials are those that are harmful to the environment or people's health. *Hazardous waste management specialists* are part of a team that identifies waste sites and remediates, or cleans up, waste.

Hazardous waste management specialists encompass a group of people who prevent spills or contamination before they happen, help to control these problems when they arise, identify contaminated sites that have existed for years, and clean up and dispose of hazardous waste.

When a polluted site is identified, specialists study the site and determine what hazardous substances are involved, how bad the damage is, and what can be done to remove the waste and restore the site. They suggest strategies for the cleanup. Once the cleanup is under way, teams of specialists ensure that the waste is removed and the site properly restored. Some specialists supervise *hazardous waste management technicians*, who do the sampling, monitoring, and testing at suspect sites.

The 10 Most Polluted Places in the World, 2006

1. Chernobyl, Ukraine
2. Dzerzhinsk, Russia
3. Haina, Dominican Republic
4. Kabwe, Zambia
5. La Oroya, Peru
6. Linfen, China
7. Maiuu Suu, Kyrgyzstan
8. Norilsk, Russia
9. Ranipet, India
10. Rudnaya Pristan/Dalnegorsk, Russia

Source: Blacksmith Institute

EXPLORING

○ Read magazines and other publications about hazardous waste management. A few publications are the *Journal of Environmental Quality* (http://jeq.scijournals.org) and the *Journal of Natural Resources and Life Sciences Education* (http://www.jnrlse.org).

○ Get involved in local chapters of citizen watchdog groups and become familiar with nearby Superfund (http://www.epa.gov/superfund) sites.

○ Ask your science teacher to set up an informational interview with a hazardous waste management specialist. Ask the following questions: What do you like most and least about your job? How did you train for this field? What advice would you give to someone interested in the career?

Education and Training

Students interested in a career in hazardous waste management should concentrate on science courses, especially chemistry, biology, and geology. Computer science, mathematics, speech, and communications courses will also be helpful.

Many employers in this field train their employees with the help of technical institutes or community colleges with courses on hazardous waste disposal. A bachelor's degree in environmental resource management; chemistry; geology; ecology; or environmental, chemical, or civil engineering also may be acceptable. Areas of expertise such as hydrology or subsurface hydrology may require a master's or doctoral degree.

Earnings

The U.S. Department of Labor reports that median earnings of hazardous materials removal workers were

Hazards of Household Waste

Americans produce 1.6 million tons of household hazardous waste per year, according to the EPA. The average home stores as much as 100 pounds of household hazardous waste. Products containing hazardous ingredients may include paints, cleaners, stains and varnishes, car batteries, motor oil, and pesticides. Sometimes people dispose of this waste improperly. They may pour it down the drain, on the ground, into storm sewers, or they may throw it in the trash. Instead, follow instructions on the label for proper disposal or take household hazardous waste to a proper collection facility.

$35,450 in 2006. Salaries ranged from less than $22,910 to more than $59,180 annually.

Hazardous waste workers employed by the private sector have middle-range salaries of $40,000 to $50,000 per year. Specialists with degrees in areas of high demand, such as toxicology or hydrology, can earn $80,000 or more, depending on seniority and certification levels.

A hazardous waste management specialist decontaminates the protective suit of another worker who has completed the cleanup of a toxic site. (Pete Saloutos, Corbis)

Outlook

Specialist jobs are fairly secure, but the hazardous waste management industry continues to change. Although the

---

Waste Treatment Technologies

○ *Biological treatment,* or *bioremediation,* uses bacteria, fungi, or algae to remove and break down the hazardous substances.

○ *Chemical reduction* uses strong reducing agents, such as sulfur dioxide, alkali salts, sulfides, and iron salts, to break down hazardous substances.

○ *Incineration* is the high-temperature burning of a waste, usually at 1,600 to 2,500 degrees Fahrenheit.

○ *Microencapsulation* is a process that coats the surface of the waste material with a thin layer of plastic or resin to prevent the material from leaching waste substances.

○ *Stabilization* reduces the mobility of hazardous substances in a waste and makes the waste easier to handle. Common stabilization agents are Portland cement, lime, fly ash, and cement kiln dust.

cleanup of sites is usually very costly and depends on funding by the government, public pressure has kept environmental funding steady over the years. The Environmental Careers Organization predicts that future job markets will revolve around waste prevention, as opposed to waste removal, neutralization, and disposal.

FOR MORE INFO

Institute of Hazardous Materials Management
11900 Parklawn Drive,
Suite 450
Rockville, MD 20852-2624
Tel: 301-984-8969
E-mail: ihmminfo@ihmm.org
http://www.ihmm.org

The following is a branch of the military that employs engineering professionals in hazardous waste management projects

U.S. Army Corps of Engineers
441 G Street NW
Washington, DC 20314-1000
Tel: 202-761-0011
http://www.usace.army.mil

Land Acquisition Professionals

What Land Acquisition Professionals Do

Land trusts are private, nonprofit groups formed to acquire lands and manage them for the public's benefit. *Land acquisition professionals* handle the transactions needed to acquire the land or rights to the land.

The first U.S. land trust, Trustees of Reservations, was formed in Boston in 1891. Concerned about development of land around the city, this group bought up some land itself and opened it to the public. Today, there are more than 1,660 trusts nationwide. They range from small, one-person trusts, to large state trusts, to national organizations that help out the smaller trusts.

Land acquisition may be someone's whole job or just one of many duties. An executive director for a small land trust, for example, may do everything from acquiring the land to managing it on a day-to-day basis. Larger, well-funded trusts and the national organizations may employ one or more people who do nothing but work on acquisitions.

There are many reasons for choosing a site to save. The trust may want to stop overly heavy grazing, farming, or recreation on the land. It may want to

Land Trust Facts

- There were more than 1,660 land trusts in the United States.
- Approximately 37 million acres were conserved—an area 16.5 times the size of Yellowstone National Park.
- California, Maine, Colorado, Montana, Virginia, New York, Vermont, New Mexico, Pennsylvania, and Massachusetts had the highest total acres conserved in land trusts.

Source: 2005 National Land Trust Census

EXPLORING

○ To learn more about this career, read publications such as the Land Trust Alliance's book *Starting a Land Trust.*

○ Contact the large national land trust organizations for career information.

○ Try to get involved with a land trust organization near you. The large national organizations should be able to provide you with the names of local groups.

keep open lands from being bought by a developer. It may want the rights to a pond or lake to clean it up and bring back native wildlife. Some trusts specialize in finding, buying, and managing lands with rare or endangered species.

After selecting the site, the acquisition professional finds out who owns the site, contacts the owner, and attempts to negotiate a sale or donation.

Education and Training

To prepare for a career in this field, take business, economics, and English courses in high school. It is also a good idea to take as many science courses as you can, such as biology and earth science.

Knowing how to negotiate is more important to an acquisition professional than any specific schooling or work background. Communication skills are also important.

Land trusts employ people from different types of educational backgrounds, from scientists to accountants. Real estate backgrounds may be useful for people wanting to focus on acquisition work. However, most acquisition professionals are trained on the job. Land acquisition professionals have bachelor's degrees in a wide variety of fields, including law, city planning, journalism, and real estate.

Earnings

Less than half of the land trusts have paid staff. However, executive directors of land trusts may earn salaries that range from $35,000 to $80,000 or more annually. Acquisition professionals employed by national groups may earn $60,000 or more per year.

To Be a Successful Land Acquisition Professional, You Should …

○ be hardworking and dedicated to the field of land conservation

○ have good communication skills

○ be organized and able to handle multiple tasks

○ be a good negotiator

○ have knowledge of land conservation options and techniques

○ be skilled in business administration, finance, and law

Outlook

The outlook for land trust work is currently brighter than that for federal land and water conservation jobs. Land trusts are going strong right now, and the entire land and water conservation segment, of which land trust and preserve management is a part, is growing at a steady rate annually. The Land Trust Alliance reports that the number of land trusts increased by 32 percent from 2000 to 2005.

FOR MORE INFO

The following is a national organization of more than 1,660 land trusts nationwide.

Land Trust Alliance
1660 L Street NW,
Suite 1100
Washington, DC 20036-5635
Tel: 202-638-4725
E-mail: info@lta.org
http://www.lta.org

For information on land conservation careers, contact

The Trust for Public Land
116 New Montgomery Street,
Fourth Floor
San Francisco, CA 94105-3603
Tel: 800-714-LAND
E-mail: info@tpl.org
http://www.tpl.org

Land Trust or Preserve Managers

What Land Trust or Preserve Managers Do

Land trusts, owned by private organizations, and preserves, government-owned lands, are protected from being developed, polluted, mined, too heavily farmed, or otherwise damaged. Hundreds of millions of acres of land and water are protected in land trusts or preserves.

Land trust and preserve managers plan for the recreational use of land and water. They take inventory of plant and animal species and protect wildlife habitats. They clean up pollution and restore damaged ecosystems. They manage forests, prairies, rangelands,

The Unlucky 13

In March 2001, the Nature Conservancy announced the creation of Prairie Wings, a program to protect, manage, and restore the grassland bird habitat of the central United States, south-central Canada, and north-central Mexico. The Conservancy named 13 species, called the "Unlucky 13," that are especially in danger:

- ○ greater prairie-chicken
- ○ lesser prairie-chicken
- ○ long-billed curlew
- ○ ferruginous hawk

- ○ lark bunting
- ○ chestnut-collared longspur
- ○ McCown's longspur
- ○ burrowing owl
- ○ Sprague's pipit
- ○ mountain plover
- ○ Baird's sparrow
- ○ Cassin's sparrow
- ○ scaled quail

and wetlands using techniques such as controlled burnings and grazing by bison or cattle.

Land trust managers work for private, nonprofit land trusts. Land trusts have become an important way for citizens concerned about the environment to take action. Land trusts get land by buying it, accepting it as a donation, or purchasing the development rights to it. There are more than 1,660 land trusts in the United States today. Land trusts can be small; one person might do everything. A few land trusts have a large, paid staff of 30 or more.

Preserve managers work for the federal government, which owns more than 700 million acres, about one-third of the United States, including forests, wilderness areas, wildlife refuges, scenic rivers, and other sites. Most of this land is managed by agencies, such as the National Park Service, U.S. Fish and Wildlife Service, and Forest Service. State and local governments may also own and manage preserve lands. The federal government employs about 75 percent of all people working in land and water conservation.

EXPLORING

○ Ask your librarian to help you find books on prairie, wetland, riparian (riverbank), and wildlife conservation, as well as land trusts and preservation.

○ Contact nonprofit land trusts or federal agencies for information about current projects in your area.

○ Ask your guidance counselor or science teacher to arrange an information interview with a land trust or preserve manager.

Education and Training

Recommended high school courses for those interested in scientific work include biology, chemistry, and physics as well as botany and ecology. All potential land trust or preserve managers can benefit from courses in business, computer science, English, and speech.

A background in biology, chemistry, and physics is important for land trust or preserve managers. A bachelor's degree in a natural science, such as zoology, biology, or botany, is recommended. A master's or a doctorate in a specialty is also a good idea, especially for government positions.

Land trusts need people who are good in business to run the trusts, raise funds, negotiate deals, and handle tax matters. The large land trust organizations also need lawyers, public relations specialists, and others.

Earnings

According to the National Association of Colleges and Employers, graduates with a bachelor's degree in environmental science received average starting salary offers of $31,366 in 2005. Salaries for conservation workers ranged from less than $20,000 to $70,000 or more annually. Conservation professionals with master's degrees and experience earn higher salaries.

Outlook

Currently, the best opportunities are with private land trusts and national land trust organizations, rather than federal

Teddy and the Environment

One of the most important people in early conservation efforts was the 26th president of the United States, Theodore (Teddy) Roosevelt. He fell in love with the West as a young man. He owned a ranch in the Dakota Territory and wrote many books about his experiences in the West.

When he became president in 1901, Roosevelt used his influence to help preserve his beloved West. He pushed conservation as part of an overall strategy for the responsible use of natural resources. His efforts fueled an increased public awareness of and support for conservation that, in turn, led to important early conservation legislation. Roosevelt's administration especially emphasized the preservation of wildlife and wilderness areas and carried out such work as the first inventory of natural resources in this country.

agencies. None of the federal agencies is expected to see big growth over the next few years. Private land trusts, however, are growing. In fact, they are the fastest-growing area of the conservation movement today. According to the Land Trust Alliance, there were more than 1,660 land trusts in 2005. LTA's 2005 National Land Trust Census reports that local and regional land trusts protected 37 million acres, 54 percent more than in 2000.

FOR MORE INFO

The following is a national organization of more than 1,660 land trusts nationwide.

Land Trust Alliance
1660 L Street NW, Suite 1100
Washington, DC 20036-5635
Tel: 202-638-4725
E-mail: info@lta.org
http://www.lta.org

The Nature Conservancy specializes in land trusts and land trust management for areas with rare or endangered species. For information about internships with, contact

The Nature Conservancy (TNC)
4245 North Fairfax Drive, Suite 100
Arlington, VA 22203-1606
Tel: 703-841-5300
E-mail: comment@tnc.org
http://nature.org

For information on opportunities for students, contact

Student Conservation Association
689 River Road
PO Box 550
Charlestown, NH 03603-0550
Tel: 603-543-1700
http://www.thesca.org

For information on land conservation careers, contact

The Trust for Public Land
116 New Montgomery Street,
Fourth Floor
San Francisco, CA 94105-3603
Tel: 800-714-LAND
E-mail: info@tpl.org
http://www.tpl.org

Marine Biologists

What Marine Biologists Do

Marine biologists study the plants and animals that live in oceans. They learn about the tens of thousands of different species that live in salt water.

To study these plants and animals in their natural environment, marine biologists take sea voyages. When they reach their destination, perhaps near a coral reef or other habitat, the scientists dive into the water to collect samples.

Because of the cold temperatures below the surface of the sea, marine biologists must wear wet suits to keep warm. They use scuba gear to help them breathe underwater. They may carry a tool, called a slurp gun, which can suck a fish into a specimen bag without hurting it. While underwater, biologists must be on the lookout for dangerous fish and mammals. They take great care not to damage the marine environment.

Marine biologists also gather specimens from tidal pools along the shore. They may collect samples at the same time of day for days at a time. They keep samples from different pools separate and carefully write down the pool's location, the types of specimens taken, and their measurements.

After they collect specimens, scientists keep them in a special portable aquarium tank on the ship. After returning to land, sometimes weeks or months later, marine biologists study the speci-

Octopus Fun Facts

- The largest octopus is the North Pacific Octopus *(Octopus dofleini)*. It can grow to over 30 feet and weighs more than 100 pounds.
- The smallest octopus is the Californian Octopus *(Octopus micropyrsus)*. It is only 3/8 inch to 1 inch in length.
- When threatened, octopuses often try to escape by releasing a cloud of purple-black ink to confuse the enemy.

mens in their laboratories. They might check the amount of oxygen in a sea turtle's bloodstream to learn how the turtles can stay underwater for so long. Or they might measure the blood chemistry of an arctic fish to discover how it can survive frigid temperatures.

Marine biologists study changing conditions of the ocean, such as temperature or chemicals that have polluted the water. They try to see how those changes affect the plants and animals that live there.

The work of these scientists is also important for improving and managing sport and commercial fishing. Through underwater exploration, marine biologists have discovered that humans are destroying the world's coral reefs. They have also charted the migration of whales and counted the decreasing numbers of certain species. They have seen dolphins being caught by accident in tuna fishermen's nets. By sharing their discoveries through written reports and research papers, marine biologists can effect meaningful change.

EXPLORING

○ Visit Web sites that focus on marine biology and oceanography. Interesting sites include MarineBio.org (http://www.marinebio.com) and Sea Grant Marine Careers (http://www.marinecareers.net/index.php).
○ Visit your local aquarium to learn about marine life and the work of marine biologists.
○ If you live near an ocean or large lake, collect shells and other specimens. Keep a notebook to record details about what you find and where.
○ Begin diving training as early as middle school. Between the ages of 10 and 14 you can earn a Junior Open Water Diver certification. This allows you to dive in the company of a certified adult. When you turn 15 you can upgrade your certification to Open Water Diver.

Education and Training

If you want to be a marine biologist, you should like math and science. Biology, botany, and chemistry classes are important to take in high school.

Although you can get a job as a marine biologist with a bachelor's degree in the subject, most marine biologists have a master's or a doctoral degree.

Earnings

Salaries vary depending on how much education and experience you have. According to the National Association of Colleges and Employers, those seeking their first job and holding bachelor's degrees in biological and life sciences received average salary offers of $31,258 in 2005. The average biologist earns about $60,000 yearly. Those who have doctorates in marine biology can earn as much as $95,000 a year. Senior scientists or full professors at universities can earn more than $110,000 a year.

Outlook

There is a lot of competition for the best jobs in marine biology. Opportunities in research are especially hard to find. If you have an advanced degree and specialized knowledge in

Aquariums on the Web

Mystic Aquarium and Institute for Exploration (Mystic, Conn.)
http://www.mysticaquarium.org

National Aquarium in Baltimore
http://www.aqua.org

New England Aquarium (Boston)
http://www.neaq.org

Seattle Aquarium
http://www.seattleaquarium.org

Shedd Aquarium (Chicago)
http://www.sheddaquarium.org

Steinhart Aquarium (San Francisco)
http://www.calacademy.org/aquarium

Waikiki Aquarium (Honolulu)
http://www.waquarium.org

Shark Fun Facts

○ There are more than 350 species of sharks.

○ Only 32 species of sharks have ever attacked people. Great white, tiger, and bull sharks are considered to be the most dangerous species.

○ Slow-growing sharks, such as the tope shark and piked dogfish, can live more than 40 years.

○ Sharks eat almost anything, including fish, crustaceans, mollusks, marine mammals, and other sharks.

mathematics and computer science you will have the best chances for employment. Changes in the Earth's environment, such as global warming, will most likely require more research, and this should create more jobs. Marine biologists should be able to find jobs managing the world's fisheries, making medicines from marine organisms, and cultivating marine food alternatives, such as seaweed and plankton.

FOR MORE INFO

For information on careers in biology, contact
American Institute of Biological Sciences
1444 I Street NW, Suite 200
Washington, DC 20005-6535
Tel: 202-628-1500
http://www.aibs.org

For information on careers, education, and publications, contact
American Society of Limnology and Oceanography

5400 Bosque Boulevard, Suite 680
Waco, TX 76710-4446
Tel: 800-929-2756
http://www.aslo.org

For information on diving instruction and certification, contact
PADI
30151 Tomas Street
Rancho Santa Margarita, CA 92688-2125
Tel: 800-729-7234
http://www.padi.com

Meteorologists

What Meteorologists Do

Meteorologists study weather conditions to forecast changes in the weather. They gather information from weather satellites above the Earth. They use this information about the atmosphere to make charts and maps that show regional and local weather conditions.

Most meteorologists specialize in one area. The largest group of specialists is called *weather forecasters*. To make their predictions, weather forecasters get weather information from many sources. In addition to weather satellites and weather radar, information is also sent from remote sensors and observers in many parts of the world. Meteorologists use advanced computer models of the world's atmosphere to help with their short-range, long-range, and local-area forecasts.

Some meteorologists, called *climatologists*, study past weather conditions of a region over a long period of time. They try to predict future weather patterns for the region.

Other meteorologists study only air currents, pollution, radiation, or hurricanes. Still others teach in colleges and universities.

The National Weather Service (NWS) employs most meteorologists. The Department of Defense and the armed forces employ the next greatest number. Other meteorologists work for weather consult-

Weather Fun Facts

○ An average-sized cloud droplet is 0.012 millimeters in diameter. A large raindrop is about 6 millimeters in diameter.

○ The largest hailstone on record in the United States was 7 inches in diameter and had a circumference of 18.75 inches. It fell in Aurora, Nebraska, on June 22, 2003.

○ Dirty snow melts faster than clean snow.

○ The largest snowflake on record was 15 inches wide and 8 inches thick. It was found at Fort Keogh, Montana, in 1887.

ing firms, airline companies, and radio and television stations.

Education and Training

If you are interested in meteorology, you should like science, especially physics and chemistry. In high school, you should take as many classes as you can in the physical sciences.

All meteorologists need at least a bachelor's degree. Many of the best jobs, though, require a master's or a doctoral degree. The best research jobs and nearly all teaching jobs in colleges and universities go to meteorologists who have advanced graduate training.

EXPLORING

○ Read books and magazines about weather.

○ Learn as much as you can about weather, from the types of clouds in the sky, to thunderstorms and tornadoes, to hurricanes, microbursts, and more.

○ Learn how to take basic weather readings such as temperature, wind speed, barometric pressure, and snow or rain totals.

Earnings

The U.S. Department of Labor reports that median annual earnings of atmospheric scientists were $77,150 in 2006. Salaries ranged from less than $39,090 to more than $119,700. The mean salary for meteorologists employed by the federal government was about $86,110 in 2006. In 2005, entry-level meteorologists with

Surf the Web

AccuWeather.com
http://www.accuweather.com

National Weather Service
http://www.nws.noaa.gov

The Weather Channel
http://www.weather.com

Weather Folklore

People have tried to predict and control the weather since the beginning of time. Here are some common weather sayings, some silly, some true.

○ If animals have an especially thick coat of fur, expect a cold winter.

○ Whatever day of the month the first snow-flake falls will signal the number of snowfalls for that winter.

○ When clouds look like chicken scratches, it will soon rain.

○ The weather on the 12 days between Christmas and January 6 foretells the weather for each of the next 12 months.

a bachelor's degree and no experience received starting salaries of $27,955 or $34,544 in government jobs, depending on college grades. Those with master's degrees started with annual salaries of $42,090 or $54,393, and those with doctorates started with $70,280. Broadcast meteorologists earn between $20,000 and $100,000 or more depending on where they work. Experienced broadcast meteorologists average $50,000 a year.

Outlook

The National Weather Service (NWS) has hired all the meteorologists it needs to staff its

FOR MORE INFO

For information on careers and education, contact
American Meteorological Society
45 Beacon Street
Boston, MA 02108-3693
Tel: 617-227-2425
E-mail: amsinfo@ametsoc.org
http://www.ametsoc.org

This government agency is concerned with describing and predicting changes in the environment, as well as managing marine and coastal resources.
National Oceanographic & Atmospheric Administration

14th Street and Constitution Avenue NW, Room 6217
Washington, DC 20230-0001
Tel: 202-482-6090
E-mail: noaa-outreach@noaa.gov
http://www.noaa.gov

For a list of schools with degree programs in meteorology or atmospheric science, visit the NWA's Web site
National Weather Association (NWA)
228 West Millbrook Road
Raleigh, NC 27609-4304
Tel: 919-845-1546
http://www.nwas.org

recently upgraded weather forecasting stations. The agency has no plans to build more weather stations or increase the number of meteorologists in existing stations for many years.

Opportunities for meteorologists in private industry, however, are expected to be better than in the federal government. Private weather consulting firms are able to provide detailed information to people working in weather-sensitive industries, such as farming, commodity investment, radio and television stations, and utilities, transportation, and construction firms.

Oceanographers

What Oceanographers Do

Oceanographers study the oceans. They perform experiments and gather information about the water, plant and animal life, and the ocean floor. They study the motion of waves, currents, and tides. They also look at water temperature, the chemical makeup of the ocean water, oil deposits on the ocean floor, and pollution levels at different depths of the oceans.

Oceanographers use several inventions specially designed for long- and short-term underwater observation. They use deep-sea equipment, such as submarines and observation tanks. Underwater devices called *bathyspheres* allow an oceanographer to stay underwater for several hours or even days. For short observations, or to explore areas such as underwater caves, scientists use deep-sea and scuba diving gear that straps onto the body to supply them with oxygen.

Most oceanographers specialize in one of four areas. Those who study ocean plants and animals are called *biological oceanographers* or *marine biologists*. *Physical oceanographers* study ocean

Did You Know?

○ Oceans cover nearly three-quarters of the planet's surface—336 million cubic miles.

○ Approximately 80 percent of all life on Earth lives in the ocean.

○ The oceans have vast stores of valuable minerals, including nickel, iron, manganese, copper, and cobalt.

○ The surface temperature of oceans ranges from about 86 degrees Fahrenheit at the equator to about 29 degrees Fahrenheit near the poles. The world's warmest water is in the Persian Gulf, where surface temperatures of 96 degrees Fahrenheit have been recorded.

temperature and the atmosphere above the water. They calculate the movement of the warm water through the oceans to help meteorologists predict weather patterns. *Geological oceanographers* study the ocean floor. They use instruments that monitor the ocean floor and the minerals found there from a far distance. *Geochemical oceanographers* study the chemical makeup of ocean water and the ocean floor. They detect oil well sites. They study pollution problems and possible chemical causes for plant and animal diseases in a particular region of the water. Geochemical oceanographers are called in after oil spills to check the level of damage to the water.

EXPLORING

○ Visit Web sites that focus on oceanography such as MarineBio.org (http://www.marinebio.com) and Sea Grant Marine Careers (http://www.marinecareers.net/index.php).
○ Read all you can about rocks, minerals, and aquatic life. If you live or travel near an oceanography research center, spend some time studying its exhibits.

Education and Training

Science courses, including geology, biology, and chemistry, and math classes, such as algebra, trigonometry, and statistics, are especially important to take in high school. Because your work

To Be a Successful Oceanographer, You Should . . .

○ have a strong interest in science, particularly the physical and earth sciences
○ have a curious nature
○ enjoy being outdoors
○ enjoy observing nature and performing experiments
○ enjoy reading, researching, and writing
○ have good communication skills
○ be able to work well with others

Oceans of the World

Name	Square Miles	Greatest Depth (feet)
Pacific	64,186,300	35,838
Atlantic	33,420,000	28,232
Indian	28,350,500	25,344
Arctic	5,105,700	18,399

The area figures for the oceans include all adjoining seas, so all the continuous salt water (the world ocean) is included. For example, the area of the Atlantic Ocean includes the Mediterranean and Black seas; the area of the Pacific Ocean includes the Bering and China seas; and the area of the Indian Ocean includes the Arabian Sea.

will involve a great deal of research and documentation, take English classes to improve your research and communication skills. In addition, take computer science classes because you will be using computers throughout your professional life.

To become an oceanographer, you will need at least a bachelor's degree in chemistry, biology, geology, or physics. For most research or teaching positions, you will need a master's degree or doctorate in oceanography.

Earnings

According to the National Association of Colleges and Employers, students graduating with a bachelor's degree in geology and related sciences were offered an average starting salary of $39,365 in 2005. According to the U.S. Department of Labor, in 2006, salaries for geoscientists (a category that includes the career of oceanographer) ranged from less than $39,740 to more than $135,950, with a median of $72,660. The average salary for experienced oceanographers working for the federal government was $86,240.

Outlook

The U.S. Department of Labor predicts that employment for oceanographers will grow more slowly than the average. The job outlook for oceanographers can change according to the world market situation. The state of the offshore oil market, for instance, can affect the demand for geophysical oceanographers. Researchers specializing in the popular field of marine biology will face competition for available positions and research funding. However, the growing interest in understanding and protecting the environment will help to create new jobs. As people confront global climate change, there will be more opportunities in oceanography, including environmental research and management, fisheries science, and marine biomedical and pharmaceutical research.

FOR MORE INFO

For information on careers, education, and publications, contact
American Society of Limnology and Oceanography
5400 Bosque Boulevard, Suite 680
Waco, TX 76710-4446
Tel: 800-929-2756
http://www.aslo.org

To purchase the booklet Education and Training Programs in Oceanography and Related Fields, *contact*
Marine Technology Society
5565 Sterrett Place, Suite 108
Columbia, MD 21044-2606
Tel: 410-884-5330
http://www.mtsociety.org

Contact this society for ocean news and information on membership.
The Oceanography Society
PO Box 1931
Rockville, MD 20849-1931
Tel: 301-251-7708
E-mail: info@tos.org
http://www.tos.org

Park Rangers

What Park Rangers Do

Park rangers protect animals and preserve forests, ponds, and other natural resources in state and national parks. They make sure rules and regulations are followed to maintain a safe environment for visitors and wildlife. They also teach visitors about the park by giving lectures and tours. The National Park Service is one of the major employers of park rangers. Park rangers may also work for other federal land and resource management agencies or state and local agencies.

One of the most important responsibilities park rangers have is the safety of others. Rangers often require visitors to register at park offices so they will know when the visitors are expected to return. Rangers carefully mark hiking trails and other areas to lessen the risk of injuries for visitors and to protect plants and animals. Rangers are trained in first aid so, if there is an accident, they are able to help visitors who have been injured.

Research and conservation efforts are also a big part of a park ranger's responsibilities. They study wildlife behavior by tagging

The Most Popular National Parks, 2006

1. **Great Smoky Mountains** (North Carolina, Tennessee)
2. **Grand Canyon** (Arizona)
3. **Yosemite** (California)
4. **Yellowstone** (Idaho, Montana, Wyoming)
5. **Olympic** (Washington)
6. **Rocky Moutain** (Colorado)
7. **Zion** (Utah)
8. **Cuyahoga Valley** (Ohio)
9. **Grand Teton** (Wyoming)
10. **Acadia** (Maine)

Source: National Park Service (by number of visits)

and following certain animals. They may investigate sources of pollution that come from outside the park. Then they develop plans to help reduce pollution to make the park a better place.

Rangers also do bookkeeping and other paperwork. They issue permits to visitors and keep track of how many people use the park. In addition, they plan recreational activities and decide how to spend the money budgeted to the park.

Education and Training

In high school, take courses in earth science, biology, mathematics, history, English, and speech. Any classes or activities that deal with plant and animal life, the weather, geography, and interpersonal relationships will be helpful.

Park rangers usually have bachelor's degrees in natural resource or recreational resource management. A degree in many other fields, such as biology or ecology, is also acceptable. Classes in forestry, geology, outdoor management, history, geography, behavioral sciences, and botany are helpful. Without a degree, you need at least three years of experience working in parks or conservation. Rangers also receive on-the-job training.

Earnings

In 2007, new rangers in the National Park Service earned between $25,623 and $33,309 annually. Rangers with some

EXPLORING

○ Read as much as you can about local, state, and national parks. The National Park Service's Web site (http://www.nps.gov) is a great place to start.

○ Get to know your local wildlife. What kind of insects, birds, fish, and other animals live in your area? Your librarian or science teacher will be able to help you find books that identify local flora and fauna.

○ You can gain valuable hands-on experience by getting involved in the Volunteers-in-Parks (VIP) program, which is sponsored by the National Park Service.

○ You also may be able to volunteer at state, county, or local parks. Universities and conservation organizations often have volunteer groups that work on research activities, studies, and rehabilitation efforts.

A National Park Service ranger in Shenandoah National Park in Virginia recommends hiking trails to visitors. (Jeff Greenberg, The Image Works)

experience earned between $31,740 and $41,262. The most experienced rangers who supervise other workers earn more than $80,000 a year. The government also sometimes provides housing to rangers who work in remote areas.

Rangers in state parks work for the state government. According to the National Association of State Park Directors, rangers employed by state parks had average starting salaries of $24,611 in 2004.

Outlook

The number of people who want to become park rangers has always been far greater than the number of positions available. The National Park Service has reported that as many as 100 people apply for each job open-

To Be a Successful Park Ranger, You Should . . .

- ○ know about protecting plants and animals
- ○ be good at explaining the natural environment
- ○ enjoy working outdoors
- ○ have a pleasant personality
- ○ be able to work with many different kinds of people
- ○ be in good physical shape
- ○ be able to enforce park rules and regulations

Our National Parks

In 1872, Congress began the U.S. National Park System with the creation of Yellowstone National Park. The National Park Service, a bureau of the U.S. Department of the Interior, was created in 1916 to manage the National Park System. At that time, the entire park system occupied less than one million acres. Today, the country's national parks cover more than 84 million acres of mountains, plains, deserts, swamps, historic sites, lakeshores, forests, rivers, battlefields, memorials, archaeological properties, and recreation areas.

ing. As a result, those interested in the field should attain the greatest number and widest variety of applicable skills possible. They may wish to study subjects they can use in other fields, such as forestry, land management, conservation, wildlife management, history, and natural sciences.

FOR MORE INFO

For information about state parks and employment opportunities, contact
National Association of State Park Directors
8829 Woodyhill Road
Raleigh, NC 27613-1134
Tel: 919-971-9300
E-mail: naspd@nc.rr.com
http://www.naspd.org

For general career information, contact the following organization
National Park Service
U.S. Department of the Interior

1849 C Street NW
Washington, DC 20240-0002
Tel: 202-208-6843
http://www.nps.gov

For information on student volunteer activities and programs, contact
Student Conservation Association
689 River Road
PO Box 550
Charlestown, NH 03603-0550
Tel: 603-543-1700
E-mail: ask-us@sca-inc.org
http://www.thesca.org

Recycling Coordinators

What Recycling Coordinators Do

Recycling coordinators manage local recycling programs. They make sure city workers or private contractors collect, sort, and process recyclable materials. They also may help find new markets for recyclables, manage a staff, and report to local authorities. Some coordinators promote recycling programs in their communities.

Today, most U.S. municipalities want to keep as much municipal solid waste (MSW) out of landfills and incinerators as possible. Landfills are places where waste is buried. They can leak hazardous substances into surrounding land and release toxic emissions. Incinerators are used to burn trash, and they, too, can release toxic emissions. When more trash is recycled, less has to be burned or buried.

Each recycling program differs according to the community, location, population, funding, and other factors. Source reduction is part of many of these plans. This means discouraging people from throwing out a lot of trash in the first place. Some cities pick up just one bag of trash per household per week and charge a fee for additional bags. To collect recyclables, some communities have drop-off points where residents can bring paper, glass, aluminum, or other materials. Others ask people to put recyclables in special

Top 10 Items to Recycle

1. aluminum
2. polyethylene terephthalate plastic bottles
3. newspapers
4. corrugated cardboard
5. steel cans
6. high-density polyethylene plastic bottles
7. glass containers
8. magazines
9. mixed paper
10. computers

Source: National Recycling Coalition

bags and throw them out with the rest of the trash. Paper, glass, and aluminum are the materials most often recycled. Other materials that can be recycled include animal waste, yard waste, appliances, wood wastes (such as shipping pallets and boxes), motor oil, scrap metal, plastic drink bottles, and tires.

Recycling coordinators are in charge of educating the public about the recycling programs that are available in their communities. They encourage people to recycle by keeping them informed about what materials can be recycled, how they should be packaged, and where and when to deposit them.

Education and Training

To prepare for this career, focus your high school studies on business, economics, English, math, and science.

A bachelor's degree in environmental studies or a related area plus business experience and proven communication

EXPLORING

○ Read industry-related magazines. Two informative publications are *Recycling Today* and *Resource Recycling*.

○ Start recycling at home. Visit the following Web sites to help you get started: National Recycling Coalition (http://www.nrc-recycle.org/consumers.aspx), Recycling For Kids (http://www.container-recycling.org/kids.htm), and paperrecyles.org (http://www.paperrecyles.org).

○ Volunteer to help with fund drives and information campaigns for a recycling organization.

○ Ask your teacher or counselor to arrange a tour of a local material recovery facility, where you can see recycling firsthand and talk with the staff there.

Harry Potter Goes Green

In 2007, Scholastic Inc., the U.S. publisher of the *Harry Potter* novels, did its part to conserve the environment. It used paper certified by the Forest Stewardship Council (FSC) to print 12 million copies of the 784-page *Harry Potter and the Deathly Hallows,* the final book in the popular series. Paper certified by the FSC is defined as being harvested from forests that are "managed in a socially and environmentally responsible" manner. At least 65 percent of the paper used for this first printing was FSC certified.

Recycling Becoming More Popular in the United States

According to *Municipal Solid Waste in the United States, 2005,* a report from the Environmental Protection Agency, the United States recycled 32 percent of its waste (or 79 million tons) in 2005—a significant increase from the 16 percent of waste recycled in 1990. Other interesting findings include:

○ Americans generated nearly 246 million tons of municipal solid waste in 2005—a decrease of almost two million tons from 2004.

○ The amount of containers and packaging that were recycled increased to 40 percent.

○ Almost 62 percent of yard waste was composted.

○ Approximately 42 million tons of paper, or 50 percent of all paper, were recycled. That's a lot of trees saved!

○ The number of landfills declined from 8,000 in 1988 to 1,654 in 2005.

skills is desirable. Some colleges and universities are developing a minor in integrated waste management. Classes include public policy, source reduction, transformation technology (composting/waste energy), and landfills.

Earnings

Salaries vary widely for recycling coordinators. Starting salaries range from $22,000 per year in smaller counties or cities to $40,000 and higher for coordinators in larger municipalities. Experienced recycling coordinators earn more than $60,000. Positions in areas with a higher cost of living, such as California, Arizona, New York, and Washington, D.C., for example, tend to pay more.

Outlook

Nationwide, the waste management and recycling industries will need more people to run recovery facilities, design new recycling technologies, and come up with new ways to use recyclables. Private businesses are also expected to hire recycling coordinators to manage in-house programs. Although the recycling industry is subject to business fluctuations, increased demand and new technologies have created a viable market for recycled materials.

FOR MORE INFO

For information on container recycling, contact
Container Recycling Institute
1776 Massachusetts Avenue NW, Suite 800
Washington, DC 20036-1904
Tel: 202-263-0999
http://www.container-recycling.org

Visit this Web site for information on recycling.
National Recycling Coalition
805 15th Street NW, Suite 425
Washington, DC 20005-2239
Tel: 202-789-1430
E-mail: info@nrc-recycle.org
http://www.nrc-recycle.org

For information on solid waste management, contact
National Solid Wastes Management Association
4301 Connecticut Avenue NW, Suite 300
Washington, DC 20008-2304
Tel: 202-244-4700
http://www.nswma.org

Renewable Energy Workers

What Renewable Energy Workers Do

Renewable energy is power or fuel that comes from wind, sunlight (solar), water (hydro), organic matter (biomass), and the Earth's internal heat (geothermal).

Top 10 Ways to Reduce Global Warming

1. Buy reusable products instead of disposable ones. Purchase products with less packaging to reduce the amount of waste. Recycle newspaper, paper, plastic, aluminum, and glass. Start a recycling program at your school.
2. Weatherproof your house to save money on heating and cooling costs. Adjust your thermostat (lower in the winter and higher in the summer) to reduce the use of fossil fuels and to save money on your utility bills.
3. Use compact fluorescent lightbulbs in place of regular lightbulbs.
4. Reduce emissions by asking your parents to drive less and walk more. Make sure that your family car is in top condition to improve gas mileage.
5. Ask your parents to purchase energy-efficient cars and appliances.
6. Use less hot water for showering and washing clothes.
7. Turn off lights, the television, radios, stereos, video games, etc. when they are not being used.
8. Plant trees to help absorb carbon dioxide and release oxygen.
9. Ask your utility company to perform an energy audit of your home.
10. Educate your family and friends about global warming and what they can do to reduce global warming and make the Earth a better place.

Source: About.com

Wind turbines generate wind energy. Wind plants, or wind farms, have many of these turbines, which can generate electricity for tens of thousands of homes. *Electrical, mechanical, and aeronautical engineers* design and test the turbines as well as the wind farms. *Meteorologists* help identify prime locations for new project sites and serve as consultants on projects. Skilled *construction workers* build the farms. *Windsmiths,* sometimes called *mechanical* or *electrical technicians,* operate and maintain the turbines and other equipment on the farm.

The most common solar energy technology today uses photovoltaic (PV) cells, which absorb sunlight and turn it into electricity. Electrical, mechanical, and *chemical engineers* work in research and development departments. *Architects,* many of whom specialize in passive solar design and construction, design solar-powered structures.

Hydropower uses the energy of flowing water to produce electricity. Electrical engineers, mechanical engineers, and technicians design, construct, and maintain hydropower projects. *Biologists* and other *environmental scientists* assess the effects of hydropower projects on wildlife and the environment.

Bioenergy is the energy stored in biomass—organic matter such as trees, straw, or corn. Bioenergy can be used directly, as in burning wood for cooking or heating purposes, or indirectly, as in producing electricity by using wood waste as a source of power. *Chemists, biochemists, biologists,* and

EXPLORING

○ Read as much as you can about renewable energy in books and on the Web.

○ Volunteering is one way to explore the renewable energy industry. You can find energy fairs or conventions in your area by contacting energy associations.

○ Many professional associations have student chapters or junior clubs. In addition to providing information about different careers in renewable energy, student chapters promote contests and offer information on scholarships and internships.

Surf the Web

Visit the following association Web sites to learn more about specific renewable energy resources:

Bioenergy
Renewable Fuels Association
http://www.ethanolrfa.org

Geothermal
Geothermal Energy Association
http://www.geo-energy.org

Hydropower
National Hydropower Association
http://www.hydro.org

Solar
American Solar Energy Society
http://www.ases.org

Wind
American Wind Energy Association
http://www.awea.org

agricultural scientists work together to find faster and less costly ways to produce bioenergy. *Farmers* and *foresters* raise and harvest crops or other sources of biomass.

Geothermal heat comes from the heat within the Earth. Water heated from geothermal energy is tapped from its underground reservoirs and used to heat buildings, grow crops, or melt snow. Geothermal energy can also be used to generate electricity. The geothermal industry employs *geologists, geochemists,* and *geophysicists* to research and locate new reservoirs. *Hydraulic engineers, reservoir engineers,* and *drillers* work together to reach and maintain the reservoir's heat supply.

Education and Training

A strong background in science and mathematics is necessary for many jobs in the renewable energy industry. Most technical jobs require at least an associate's or bachelor's degree. Courses of study range from environmental science and mathematics to architecture and meteorology. Research and development workers usually have a bachelor's or master's degree in electrical, chemical, or mechanical engineering. Some scientists have graduate degrees in engineering or the sciences (such as biology, physics, or chemistry).

A windsmith at a wind farm repairs a turbine.
(National Renewable Energy Laboratory)

However, you need not be technically gifted in science and math in order to succeed in the renewable energy industry. Computer classes are useful for workers who run design programs, organize research, and maintain basic office records. Finance, accounting, communications, and English classes will be helpful to anyone who is interested in working in the business end of the industry. Taking a foreign language is highly useful since a majority of renewable energy companies are located outside of the United States.

Earnings

Very little salary information is available for specific jobs in each subindustry. However, a 2001 survey by the Association of Energy Engineers found that the average annual salary of an engineer employed in the energy industry was $70,459.

Annual salaries for nontechnical workers vary according to the position, type and size of the employer, and job

FOR MORE INFO

For information on careers, employment opportunities, and industry surveys, contact
Association of Energy Engineers
4025 Pleasantdale Road, Suite 420
Atlanta, GA 30340-4260
Tel: 770-447-5083
http://www.aeecenter.org

For general information on the renewable energy industry, contact
Energy Efficiency and Renewable Energy
U.S. Department of Energy
Mail Stop EE-1
Washington, DC 20585
Tel: 877-337-3463
http://www.eere.energy.gov

For more information on renewable energy, careers, and internships, contact
National Renewable Energy Laboratory
1617 Cole Boulevard
Golden, CO 80401-3393
Tel: 303-275-3000
http://www.nrel.gov

responsibilities. A typical administrative position would probably pay salaries ranging from $20,000 to $50,000. Those employed by nonprofit organizations tend to earn slightly less than their corporate counterparts.

Outlook

The wind industry is the fastest-growing sector of the renewable energy industry, and rapid growth is expected in the next decade, especially for windsmiths, engineers, meteorologists, electricians, and other technical workers.

Solar energy use is already well established in high-value markets such as remote power, satellites, and communications. The manufacturing of PV cell systems will present many employment opportunities.

Growth in the hydropower industry will be limited because most potential sites for hydropower projects have already been tapped.

Bioenergy is experiencing steady growth, with good employment opportunities for chemists, engineers, and other agricultural scientists.

Employment opportunities in geothermal energy are greatest in the West for the direct use, or drilling, of geothermal energy, and in the Midwest for geothermal heat pumps.

Soil Conservationists and Technicians

What Soil Conservationists and Technicians Do

Soil conservationists develop conservation plans to help people use their land in the best way while still following government conservation regulations. They suggest plans to conserve and reclaim soil, preserve or restore wetlands and other rare ecological areas, rotate crops for increased yields and soil conservation, reduce water pollution, and restore or increase wildlife populations. They assess the land users' needs, costs, maintenance requirements, and the life expectancy of various conservation practices. They plan design specifications using survey and field information, technical guides, and engineering field manuals. Soil conservationists also give talks to various organizations to educate land users and the public in general about how to conserve and restore soil and water resources.

Soil conservation technicians work more directly with land users by putting the ideas and plans of the conservationist into action. They take soil samples

The Dirt on Soil

Soil is a combination of plant, animal, mineral, and other matter. It contains sand, silt, and clay particles, as well as water, air, and many different microorganisms.

Soil provides all but three of the 16 nutrients that plants need to grow. Soil also releases these nutrients into streams and oceans, where fish and other aquatic life benefit from them.

Soil cleans water. Nearly all freshwater travels over or through soil before entering rivers, lakes, and aquifers. The processes that take place in the upper layers of soil help remove many impurities from the water and kill some disease-causing organisms. Soil helps prevent flooding by soaking up large amounts of rain and distributing it to bodies of water over days, months, or years.

Source: Soil and Water Conservation Society

EXPLORING

○ Join a chapter of the National 4-H Council (http://www.fourhcouncil. edu) or National FFA Organization (http://www.ffa.org).

○ Visit the following Web sites to learn more about soil conservation: The Field Museum Underground Adventure (http://www.fmnh.org/ ua/default.htm), The Pedosphere and Its Dynamics (http://www. pedosphere.com), and Just for Kids: Soil Biological Communities (http:// www.blm.gov/nstc/soil/Kids).

○ Science courses that include lab sections and mathematics courses that focus on practical problem solving will also give you a feel for this kind of work.

\and help landowners select, install, and maintain measures that conserve and improve the soil and other related resources.

When a soil conservationist designs a new conservation plan for a landowner, technicians inspect the different phases of the project as it is constructed. They might inspect ponds, structures, dams, tile, outlet terraces, and animal waste control facilities.

Soil conservation technicians mainly work with farmers and agricultural concerns. They also work with land developers and local governments to prevent soil erosion and preserve wetlands.

Education and Training

To prepare for a career as a soil conservationist, be sure to take as many science classes as possible, including earth science, biology, and chemistry. If your high school offers agriculture classes, enroll in any that relate to land use, crop production, and soils. Also take math classes such as algebra, geometry, and trigonometry.

Soil conservationists hold bachelor's degrees in areas such as general agriculture, range management, crop or soil science, forestry, and agricultural engineering. If you want to teach or work in a research position, you will need further graduate-level education in a natural resources field. Though government jobs do not necessarily require a college degree (a combination of appropriate experience and education can serve as substitute), a college education can make you more desirable for a position.

Soil conservation technicians need at least a high school diploma. Courses in mathematics, speech, writing, chemistry, and biology are important. Courses in vocational agriculture, which is the study of farming as an occupation, are also helpful. Some technical institutes and junior or community colleges offer an associate's degree in soil conservation.

Earnings

The majority of soil conservationists and technicians work for the federal government. In 2005, the average annual salary for soil conservationists employed by the federal government was $60,671, according to the *Occupational Outlook Handbook*. The starting salary for those with bachelor's degrees employed by the federal government was between $24,677 and $30,567 in 2005, depending on academic achievement. Those with master's degrees earned a higher starting salary of between $37,390 and $45,239, and with a doctorate, $54,221.

The U.S. Department of Labor reports that median earnings for soil and plant scientists were $56,080 in 2006. Some scientists earned less than $33,650, while others earned $93,460 or more annually.

The U.S. Department of Labor reports that median earnings for forest and conservation technicians (including those who specialize in soil science) were $30,880 in 2006. Salaries ranged from less than $22,450 to more than $49,380 annually.

NRCS to the Rescue

After the Dust Bowl (a series of devastating dust storms in the U.S. in the 1930s caused by overfarming and other factors), Congress established the Natural Resource Conservation Service (NRCS) of the U.S. Department of Agriculture in 1935. The job of reclaiming the land through wise conservation practices was not an easy one because more than 800 million tons of topsoil had already been blown away by the winds.

The salaries of conservationists and technicians working for private firms or agencies are about the same as those paid by the federal government. Earnings at the state and local levels are usually lower.

Outlook

The *Occupational Outlook Handbook* reports that employment within the field of soil science is expected to grow more slowly than the average. The federal government employs most soil conservationists and technicians, so employment opportunities rely heavily on government spending. Most of America's cropland has suffered from some sort of erosion, so soil conservation professionals will be needed to help prevent a dangerous depletion of fertile soil.

FOR MORE INFO

Contact the NRCS for information on government soil conservation careers. Its Web site has information on volunteer opportunities.
Natural Resources Conservation Service (NRCS)
U.S. Department of Agriculture
PO Box 2890
Washington, DC 20013-2890
http://www.nrcs.usda.gov

For information on soil science and conservation, contact
National Society of Consulting Soil Scientists
PO Box 1724
Sandpoint, ID 83864-0901

Tel: 800-535-7148
E-mail: info2007@nscss.com
http://www.nscss.org

Soil and Water Conservation Society
945 SW Ankeny Road
Ankeny, IA 50023-9723
Tel: 515-289-2331
http://www.swcs.org

For the career brochure Soils Sustain Life, *contact*
Soil Science Society of America
677 South Segoe Road
Madison, WI 53711-1086
Tel: 608-273-8080
http://www.soils.org

Soil Scientists

What Soil Scientists Do

Soil is one of our most important natural resources. It provides the nutrients necessary to grow food for hundreds of millions of people. To use soil wisely and keep it from washing away or being damaged, experts must analyze it and find the best ways to manage it. *Soil scientists* are these experts. Soil scientists collect soil samples and study their chemical and physical characteristics. They study how soil responds to fertilizers and other farming practices. This helps farmers decide what types of crops to grow on certain soils.

Words to Learn

aeration porosity the fraction of the volume of soil that is filled with air at any given time

blowout a small area from which soil material has been removed by wind

creep slow mass movement of soil and soil material down steep slopes primarily under the influence of gravity, but aided by saturation with water and by alternate freezing and thawing

dunes wind-built ridges and hills of sand formed in the same manner as snowdrifts

gytta peat consisting of plant and animal residues from standing water

karst topography with caves, sinkholes, and underground drainage that is formed in limestone and other rocks by dissolution

macronutrient a nutrient found in high concentrations in a plant

scarp a cliff or steep slope along the margin of a plateau

Soil scientists study a soil sample in a laboratory.
(Rob Flynn, USDA, Agricultural Research Service)

EXPLORING

○ Visit the following Web sites to learn more about soil conservation: The Field Museum Underground Adventure (http://www. fmnh.org/ua/default.htm), The Pedosphere and Its Dynamics (http://www.pedosphere.com), and Just for Kids: Soil Biological Communities (http://www.blm. gov/nstc/soil/Kids).

○ Join a chapter of the National 4-H Council (http://www.fourhcouncil. edu) or National FFA Organization (http://www.ffa.org).

○ If you live in an agricultural community, look for part-time or summer work on a farm or ranch.

Soil scientists do much of their work outdoors. They go to fields to take soil samples. They spend many hours meeting with farmers and discussing ways to avoid soil damage.

Soil scientists work for agricultural research laboratories, crop production companies, and other organizations. They also work with road departments to advise them about the quality and condition of the soil over which roads will be built. Some soil scientists may travel to foreign countries to conduct research and observe the way other scientists treat the soil. Many also teach at colleges, universities, and agricultural schools.

Education and Training

To be a soil scientist, you need a solid background in mathematics and science, especially the physical and earth sciences.

The best way to become a soil scientist is to go to college and earn a bachelor's degree. Then you should go on to earn a master's degree in agricultural or soil science. A degree in biology, physics, or chemistry might also be acceptable, but you should take some courses in agriculture. With a bachelor's degree in agricultural science, you can get some nonresearch jobs, but you will not be able to advance very far. Most research and teaching positions require a doctorate.

Earnings

According to the U.S. Department of Labor, median earnings for soil and plant scientists were $56,080 in 2006. Salaries ranged from less than $33,650 to more than $93,460. Federal salaries for soil scientists were higher. In 2006, they had median earnings of $67,530 a year. Government earnings depend in large part on levels of experience and education. Those with doctorates and a great deal of experience may qualify for higher government positions, with salaries ranging from $80,000 to $100,000.

Outlook

Agricultural problems will continue to be an issue in the United States in the coming years. Soil scientists should find plenty of job opportunities. There have not been as many agricultural students in the past few years as there were in the past, which should create more job openings.

FOR MORE INFO

For information on agricultural careers, contact
American Society of Agronomy
677 South Segoe Road
Madison, WI 53711-1086
Tel: 608-273-8080
E-mail: headquarters@agronomy.org
http://www.agronomy.org

For information on soil science and conservation, contact
National Society of Consulting Soil Scientists

PO Box 1724
Sandpoint, ID 83864-0901
Tel: 800-535-7148
E-mail: info2007@nscss.com
http://www.nscss.org

For the career brochure Soils Sustain Life, *contact*
Soil Science Society of America
677 South Segoe Road
Madison, WI 53711-1086
Tel: 608-273-8080
http://www.soils.org

Soil scientists will be able to find jobs with private companies, such as seed, fertilizer, and farm equipment companies, as well as with government agencies. There will be more opportunities in teaching and in research.

Glossary

accredited approved as meeting established standards for providing good training and education. This approval is usually given by an independent organization of professionals.

apprentice a person who is learning a trade by working under the supervision of a skilled worker. Apprentices often receive classroom instruction in addition to their supervised practical experience.

associate's degree an academic rank or title granted by a community or junior college or similar institution to graduates of a two-year program of education beyond high school.

bachelor's degree an academic rank or title given to a person who has completed a four-year program of study at a college or university. Also called an undergraduate degree or baccalaureate.

career an occupation for which a worker receives training and has an opportunity for advancement.

certified approved as meeting established requirements for skill, knowledge, and experience in a particular field. People are certified by the organization of professionals in their field.

college a higher education institution that is above the high school level.

community college a public or private two-year college attended by students who do not usually live at the college. Graduates of a community college receive an associate's degree and may transfer to a four-year college or university to complete a bachelor's degree.

diploma a certificate or document given by a school to show that a person has completed a course or has graduated from the school.

distance education a type of educational program that allows students to take classes and complete their education by mail or the Internet.

doctorate the highest academic rank or title granted by a graduate school to a person who has completed a program after having received a master's degree.

fringe benefit a payment or benefit to an employee in addition to regular wages or salary. Examples of fringe benefits include a pension, a paid vacation, and health or life insurance.

graduate school a school that people may attend after they have received their bachelor's degree. People who complete an educational program at a graduate school earn a master's degree or a doctorate.

intern an advanced student (usually one with at least some college training) in a professional field who is employed in a job that is intended to provide supervised practical experience for the student.

internship 1. the position or job of an intern. 2. the period of time when a person is an intern.

junior college a two-year college that offers courses like those in the first half of a four-year college program. Graduates of a junior college usually receive an associate's degree and may transfer to a four-year college or university to complete a bachelor's degree.

liberal arts the subjects covered by college courses that develop broad general knowledge rather than specific occupational skills. The liberal arts are often considered to include philosophy, literature and the arts, history, language, and some courses in the social sciences and natural sciences.

major (in college) the academic field in which a student specializes and receives a degree.

master's degree an academic rank or title granted by a graduate school to a person who has completed a one- or two-year program after having received a bachelor's degree.

pension an amount of money paid regularly by an employer to a former employee after he or she retires from working.

scholarship a gift of money to a student to help him or her pay for further education.

social studies courses of study (such as civics, geography, and history) that deal with how human societies work.

starting salary annual pay for a newly hired employee. The starting salary is usually a smaller amount than is paid to a more experienced worker.

technical college a private or public college offering two- or four-year programs in technical subjects. Technical colleges offer courses in both general and technical subjects and award associate's degrees and bachelor's degrees.

undergraduate a student at a college or university who has not yet received a degree.

undergraduate degree See **bachelor's degree**.

union an organization whose members are workers in a particular industry or company. The union works to gain better wages, benefits, and working conditions for its members. Also called a labor union or trade union.

vocational school a public or private school that offers training in one or more skills or trades.

wage money that is paid in return for work done, especially money paid on the basis of the number of hours or days worked.

Index of Job Titles

Browse and Learn More

Books

Arthus-Bertrand, Yann. *The Future of the Earth: An Introduction to Sustainable Development for Young Readers*. New York: Harry N. Abrams, 2004.

Blobaum, Cindy. *Geology Rocks!: 50 Hands-On Activities to Explore the Earth*. Nashville, Tenn.: Williamson, 1999.

Challen, Paul C. *Environmental Disaster Alert!* New York: Crabtree, 2004.

Claybourne, Anna, Gillian Doherty, and Rebecca Treays. *Encyclopedia of Planet Earth*. Tulsa, Okla.: Usborne, 2000.

Cohen, Judith Love, and Lee Rathbone. *You Can Be a Woman Meteorologist*. Marina del Rey, Calif.: Cascade Pass Inc., 2002.

David, Laurie, and Cambria Gordon. *Down-to-Earth Guide To Global Warming*. New York: Scholastic, 2007.

Donald, Rhonda Lucas. Air Pollution. New York: Children's Press, 2002.

———. *Endangered Animals*. New York: Children's Press, 2002.

———. *The Ozone Layer*. New York: Children's Press, 2002.

———. *Recycling*. New York: Children's Press, 2002.

———. *Water Pollution*. New York: Children's Press, 2002.

Heitzmann, William Ray. *Opportunities in Marine Science and Maritime Careers*. New York: McGraw-Hill, 2006.

Jefferis, David. *Green Power: Eco-Energy Without Pollution*. New York: Crabtree, 2006.

Kellert, Stephen, and Matthew Black. *The Encyclopedia of the Environment*. New York: Franklin Watts, 1999.

Legault, Marie-Anne. *Scholastic Atlas of Weather*. New York: Scholastic, 2004.

McAlary, Florence, and Judith Love Cohen. *You Can Be a Woman Marine Biologist.* Rev. ed. Marina del Rey, Calif.: Cascade Pass, Inc., 2001.

McMillan, Beverly, and John A. Musick. *Oceans.* New York: Simon & Schuster Children's, 2007.

Morgan, Sally. *From Windmills to Hydrogen Fuel Cells: Discovering Alternative Energy.* Portsmouth, N.H.: Heinemann, 2007.

Needham, Bobbe. *Ecology Crafts For Kids: 50 Great Ways To Make Friends With Planet Earth.* New York: Sterling, 1998.

Passero, Barbara. *Energy Alternatives.* Farmington Hills, Mich.: Greenhaven Press, 2006.

Peterson's Summer Opportunities for Kids & Teenagers. 24th ed. Lawrenceville, N.J.: Peterson's, 2006.

Tocci, Salvatore. *Experiments With Weather.* New York: Children's Press, 2004.

Williams, Linda. *Earth Sciences Demystified.* New York: McGraw-Hill Professional, 2004.

Web Sites

About.com: Environmental Issues
http://environment.about.com/mbody.htm

American Library Association: Great Web Sites for Kids
http://www.ala.org/greatsites

Backyard Conservation
http://www.nacdnet.org/education/backyard/

Backyard Nature
http://www.backyardnature.net

BBC Science & Nature
http://www.bbc.co.uk/nature

Canon Envirothon
http://www.envirothon.org

EcoKids Online
http://www.ecokids.ca

Environmental Education for Kids!

http://www.dnr.state.wi.us/eek

The Green Squad

http://www.nrdc.org/greensquad

Ground Water Adventurers

http://www.groundwateradventurers.org

Just for Kids: Soil Biological Communities

http://www.blm.gov/nstc/soil/Kids

Kids For a Clean Environment

http://www.kidsface.org

National Geographics Kids

http://kids.nationalgeographic.com

National Park Service: Nature and Science

http://www.nature.nps.gov

The Nature Conservancy

http://www.nature.org

PBS: American Field Guide

http://www.pbs.org/americanfieldguide

Underground Adventure

http://www.fieldmuseum.org/undergroundadventure

U. S. Environmental Protection Agency: Resources for Waste Education

http://www.epa.gov/epaoswer/education/index.htm

World Wildlife Fund

http://www.worldwildlife.org